Steck Vaughn

Social Studies

Level C

Living
IN OUR
Communities

PROGRAM CONSULTANTS

Sonya Abbye Taylor, Senior Associate
Professional Development Network, Inc.
(Education Consultant)
New Rochelle, N.Y.
and
Field Supervisor and Instructor
Manhattanville College
Purchase, N.Y.

Barbara C. Donahue, Principal
Burlington County Special Services School District
Westampton, N.J.

Harcourt Achieve

Rigby • Saxon • Steck-Vaughn

www.HarcourtAchieve.com
1.800.531.5015

ACKNOWLEDGMENTS

Photo Credits: P.5 ©Ray Hendley/Index Stock; p.6 ©Rhoda Sidney/PhotoEdit; p.7 ©Michal Heron; p.8 ©Tom Bean/CORBIS; pp.9, 10, 11 ©Michal Heron; p.12 ©The Museum of Modern Art, New York/Art Resource; p.14 ©Berenholtz/CORBIS; p.15 (left) ©Joan Menschenfreund, (right) Michal Heron; p.17 (left) ©Vermont Agency of Development & Community Affairs, (right) ©Ron Dahlquist/Superstock; p.19 (right) ©Gus Boyd/Photo Researchers, (bottom) ©K. Preuss/The Image Works; p.20 ©F. Prenzel/Animals Animals; p.23 ©Ray Hendley/Index Stock; p.24 ©Jeff Greenberg/PhotoEdit; p.25 ©Ellis Herwig/Stock Boston; p.27 ©Michal Heron; p.28 ©Dick Keen/ Unicorn Stock Photos; pp.31, 32 ©Michal Heron; p.33 ©Wes Thompson/CORBIS; p.34 ©Joan Menschenfreund; p.35 ©Courtesy Bostonian Society/Old State House; p.37 ©Index Stock; p.39 ©J. Pickerell/The Image Works; p.40 (both) ©Patrick R. Dunn; p.41 ©Timothy Eagan/Woodfin Camp & Associates; p.45 ©Joan Menschenfreund; p.46 ©Michal Heron; p.47 Courtesy of the Bancroft Library, University of California, Berkeley; p.48 ©National Portrait Gallery, Smithsonian Institution/Art Resource, NY; p.51 ©Jeff Greenberg/PhotoEdit; p.52 ©Jean Higgins/Unicorn Stock Photos; p.53 ©Michal Heron; p.55 ©W. Hill/The Image Works p.56 ©Michal Heron; p.57 (left) ©Roger Ball/CORBIS; p.59 ©Sophia Smith Collection, Smith College; p.61 ©David Barnes/Photo Researchers; p.66 (left) ©Bruno Barbey/Magnum Photos, (bottom) ©Marc & Evelyn Bernheim/Woodfin Camp & Associates; p.69 ©Jean Higgins/Unicorn Stock Photos; p.70 ©Bob Daemmrich/The Image Works; p.71 ©Nancy Sheehan/PhotoEdit; p.75 ©National Portrait Gallery, Smithsonian Institution/Art Resource, NY; p.77 ©Richard Hutchings; p.79 (bottom left) ©Myrleen Ferguson Cate/PhotoEdit, (bottom right) ©Michal Heron; pp.80, 81 ©Michal Heron; p.82 (both) ©U.S. Department of Commerce, Bureau of the Census; p.84 ©Michael Newman/PhotoEdit; p.87 ©Georgia Department of Industry, Trade, & Tourism; p.88 (left) ©Jean Claude Lejuene/Stock Boston, (bottom) ©Jacqueline Durand; p.93 ©Bob Daemmrich/The Image Works; p.94 ©Donovan Reese/Getty Images; p.102 ©National Portrait Gallery, Smithsonian Institution/Art Resource, NY; p.104 ©detail of Benjamin Franklin Reinhart "The Emigrant Train Bedding Down for the Night", 1867 Oil on canvas 40x70 in., Corcoran Gallery of Art, Washington, D.C.; pp.106, 107, 108 Nebraska State Historical Society Photograph Collections; p.109 ©Michal Heron; p.111 ©Comstock; p.112 ©Jim Selzle; p.113 ©Gilmore J. Dufresne/Uniphoto/ImageState; p.115 (middle) ©Nebraska State Historical Society Photograph Collections, (bottom) ©Dave Schaefer/Uniphoto/ImageState; p.116 ©Superstock; p.120 ©Bill Auth/ Uniphoto/ImageState; p.121 ©Nick Nicholson; p.122 ©J. Barnell/Shostal Superstock; p.124 ©Louise Goldman/ Photo Researchers; p.125 (top right) ©Steve Vidler/Superstock, (middle right) ©Sheryl McNee/Getty Images, (bottom) ©Jon Ortner; p.126 ©Westenberger/Gamma-Liaison/Getty Images; p.130 ©Ariel Skelley/CORBIS; p.131 ©Evan Agonstini/Gamma-Liaison/Getty Images; p. ©May 1975 photo by Greg White/TxDOT; p.133 ©Lawrence⁻ Migdale/Stock Boston; p.136 ©Bill Auth/Uniphoto/ImageState.

Additional photography by Getty Images Royalty Free.

ISBN: 0-7398-9220-7

12 2331 17

4500356823

Contents

What Is a Community?

People live together in towns and cities all over the world. What is the name of the place where you live? Is it a town? Is it a city?

Unit 1 of this book will help you find answers to questions like these about places where people live together.

- In what different kinds of places do people live?

- Why do people all over the world live together in groups?

UNIT PROJECT

Start a team project. Find out what makes your community a special place. Make a bulletin board display to show what you find. Work on your project as you read Unit 1.

People and Places

Look at the photograph. These people are buying handmade items from American Indians. These people live in Santa Fe, New Mexico. They are part of a **community.** A community is a place where people live, work, and play.

People Need Communities

Why do people live in communities? People can help one another when they live together. People also live together so they can get things done. Some people—like you—go to school. Some build roads. Others run stores. One person or one family cannot do all these things alone.

Think of two reasons why people live in communities. Write your answers here.

Were thay work.

Were thar family.

This market is in Santa Fe. American Indian craftspeople make and sell beautiful handmade items.

This is Angela Carrillo. She lives in Santa Fe. It is the **capital** of New Mexico. A capital is a city. The government of a state meets there. New Mexico is one of the 50 states that make up our country. There are many different communities in each state.

Look at the map below. It shows the state of New Mexico. **Symbols** on the map stand for real things. The **map key** tells what each symbol stands for. A **compass rose** shows directions.

Find the map key. What does the first symbol stand for? Write your answer here.

_____

Find the same symbol on the map. Circle it and the city it stands for.

Find the second symbol and circle it on the map.

Circle the compass rose. Is Santa Fe north or south of Albuquerque? Write your answer here.

_____

Angela lives in Santa Fe, New Mexico.

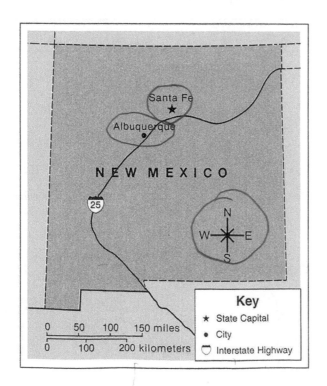

7

Santa Fe is one of the oldest cities in the United States. It has many beautiful, old buildings. These buildings make Santa Fe different from other communities in our country. What things make your community different?

Look at the map below. This map shows some buildings in Santa Fe. How does a map show how far apart real places are? The map has a **distance scale.** A distance scale is a measuring line that helps you find distances.

Find the distance scale in the map key. Circle it. Draw a line from the cathedral to the Wheelwright Museum. Use a ruler to measure this line on the distance scale. About how far is the cathedral from the museum? Write your answer here.

about 1 mile

Buildings are an important part of every community. People work and live and learn in a community's buildings.

Most of Santa Fe's buildings look old.

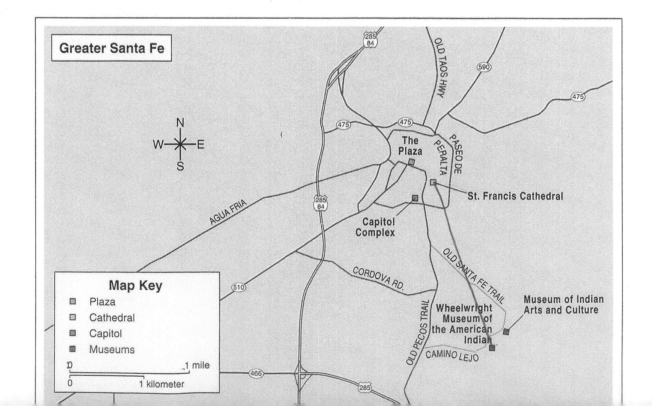

Greater Santa Fe

285 84
OLD TAOS HWY
590
475
475
475
The Plaza
PASEO DE PERALTA
St. Francis Cathedral
285 84
AGUA FRIA
Capitol Complex
OLD SANTA FE TRAIL
CORDOVA RD.
510
Museum of Indian Arts and Culture
OLD PECOS TRAIL
Wheelwright Museum of the American Indian
CAMINO LEJO
466
285

Map Key
- Plaza
- Cathedral
- Capitol
- Museums

0 _____ 1 mile
0 _____ 1 kilometer

(above) Mrs. Carrillo studies plans for a new building. She likes her work.
(below) Angela's family likes living in Santa Fe.

Looking at Life in a Community

Here is Angela's family. The Carrillos **depend on** their community for many things. When you depend on something, you put your trust in it. Santa Fe depends on the Carrillo family too.

Angela's mother works for the city. Her job is to make sure new buildings will not spoil the old look of Santa Fe. Why do you think this job is important to the community?

Why would people want their city to have a special look? Write your answer here.

To keep it o _____

_____

Mr. Carrillo's job is to check the highways in Santa Fe and in the whole state of New Mexico. He helps decide which highways need repairs. He helps keep the roads and streets safe. The people of Santa Fe depend on Mr. Carrillo's work. So do the other communities of the state.

9

Depending on One Another

Angela's family depends on the stores and other **businesses** in the community. A business is a store or other place where people buy and sell things. There, the Carrillos buy the things they need and want. The stores and businesses depend on people like the Carrillos, too. Stores need people to buy the things they sell.

Look at the pictures. Circle what the Carrillos are buying in each picture. Name each place in which the Carrillos are buying something. Write your answers on the lines under the pictures.

1. _____

_____

2. _____

_____

3. _____

_____

Places People Share

People in a community share some places. These are called **public** places. Public places are for everyone to use.

Angela and her family often use the library in Santa Fe. Sometimes they visit the city's parks. Angela goes to a public school in her community, too.

Find the picture that shows Angela at the library. Circle something in the picture that tells you she is in a library.

(above) The Carrillos often use public places. Angela visits the library. (below, left) Here, the family visits a museum in their community. (below, right) Angela learns how to use a bow and arrow at one of Santa Fe's parks.

UNIT PROJECT TIP

Work with your team. Gather pictures and facts about your community. You can draw pictures or cut them from newspapers or booklets. What special buildings are found in your community? What kinds of businesses are there in your community?

Pretend you are going to draw a picture of your community. What would you show? The African American artist Jacob Lawrence asked himself this question all the time. For more than 60 years, he painted the people and places where he lived.

Jacob Lawrence began painting in the 1930s. These were hard times for most Americans. At that time Lawrence lived in New York City. Many of his first paintings show what life was like then. He painted people who lived in a part of the city called Harlem. Most of these people were African Americans. Lawrence became one of the first artists to paint pictures in the streets of Harlem.

Jacob Lawrence lived in Seattle, Washington, when he died in 2000. His paintings hang in museums all over the United States. Some of his most famous paintings show the lives of other important African Americans.

Circle something in the painting that tells about learning.

The Jacob Lawrence ptg: "In the north the negro had better educational facilities" Panel No. 58 from the series: The Migration of the Negro. (1940–41)

12

CHAPTER ✓ CHECKUP

Finish each sentence. Circle the letter of the correct answer.

1. People live, work, and play in a
   a. highway.
   b. community.
   c. business.
   d. supermarket.

2. People live together in communities mostly because they
   a. like to go to museums.
   b. can help one another.
   c. want to save old buildings.
   d. have to repair highways.

3. The government of a state meets in
   a. New Mexico.
   b. the largest city.
   c. every community.
   d. the capital.

4. In this country, every community is one of many in a
   a. state.
   b. capital.
   c. building.
   d. museum.

5. People buy what they need from
   a. states and capitals.
   b. churches and libraries.
   c. stores and businesses.
   d. cities and towns.

6. Two public places are
   a. houses and bands.
   b. stores and homes.
   c. bows and arrows.
   d. schools and parks.

THINKING AND WRITING How do you and your community depend on each other?

_____

_____

_____

_____

_____

Communities and Their Geography

Chicago is a large city that depends on Lake Michigan for a variety of uses.

Where is your community? Is it in a place that is hilly? Is it in a flat place? Is it by the ocean? Is it hot or cold, rainy or dry?

It is important to know about your community's land and **weather.** Weather is how hot or cold and how wet or dry it is. Weather is an important part of your community.

Riches of the Land

This picture shows Chicago, Illinois. Chicago is on the shore of Lake Michigan. Do you see the lake?

> **Draw an arrow that points to one of Chicago's tall buildings.**

Many communities began along lakes, rivers, and oceans. That's because water is important to communities. People use water in many ways. They drink it, wash with it, and travel on it. They even use it to make electricity and other kinds of power.

 Think of a place in your community where there is water. Write its name here.

_____

(left) Logging communities grow where there are plenty of trees. (below) Farming communities grow where the soil is good.

There is something else people use water for—fun! People in Chicago swim in and sail on Lake Michigan. Is there a place in your community where you can do these things?

Water is a **natural resource.** A resource is something people need and use. A natural resource comes from nature. Other natural resources are important to communities, too.

The logs shown in the photograph above come from a forest in the western state of Washington. Forests are a natural resource. Wood from the forests is needed by communities all over the country. Is the home you live in made of wood?

Good soil is another natural resource. Do you know why? Farmers need good soil to grow their crops. The food that farmers grow is needed by communities, too.

What is one natural resource found in your community? Write your answer here.

15

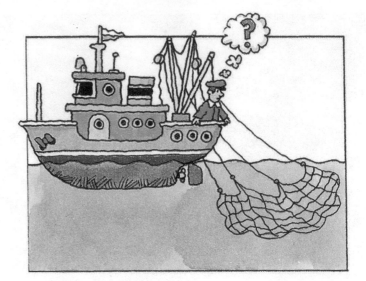

Fish are a natural resource, too. In some communities near the sea, people make a living by fishing. The fish are used for food and for other things that people need. Did you know that fish oil is used to make goods such as paint and ink?

 Look at the picture at the top of the page. Circle what the fisherman will use to catch the fish.

Minerals are also natural resources. A mineral is something people get by mining or digging in the ground. Some minerals are rocks, gold, and oil. The picture below shows how oil is drilled from the ground.

Put an X where the oil is mined.

Circle two things that use gas and oil.

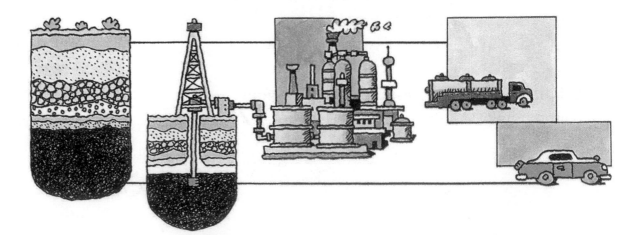

Rain or Shine

What is the weather like in your community? The kind of weather a place has over a period of time is called **climate.** Climate, like natural resources, is important to communities.

Some communities have mostly sunny and warm weather. One such community is Honolulu, Hawaii. Many people visit Honolulu because of its climate. The city has lots of hotels and restaurants for its visitors.

Find the picture of Honolulu below. Circle one natural resource.

Some communities in Colorado and Utah have lots of snow in the winter. Many people come to these states to ski.

Name two kinds of climate that can help a community. Write your answer here.

_____

_____

(left) The states of Colorado and Utah have a good climate for snow sports. (right) Sunny Honolulu is the largest city in Hawaii.

Shapes of the Land

Look at the map of North Carolina. Why is North Carolina shown in two colors? The answer is that it has two kinds of **landforms.** Landforms are the shapes of the land.

This map shows the different kinds of land in North Carolina. The green part of the map shows **plains.** Plains are flat land. More of the world's communities are found on plains than in the **mountains.** Mountains are very high land. The orange part on the map shows mountains. It is easier to build communities on plains.

Look at the map. Put a ✔ in front of the names of two mountain groups.

The map shows many of the communities in North Carolina. Where are they found? Write _plains_ or _mountains_ here.

_____

Plains make good farmland.

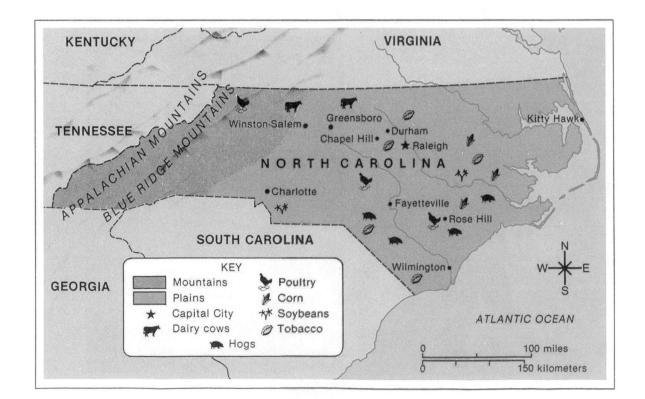

18

Mountains and plains are two kinds of landforms. Do you live near a hill? Hills are landforms, too. Many communities lie in the low land between mountains. That kind of landform is called a **valley.** A very deep valley with steep walls is called a **canyon.**

Name two landforms. Write your answer here.

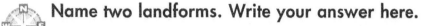

Landforms make a difference to a community. The work that people do may depend on landforms. The Navajo people in the picture below farm and raise goats and sheep. That's because goats and sheep live well in the canyons of Navajo land.

Landforms can make a difference in other ways, too. San Francisco is a city with many steep hills. It is famous for its cable cars, a kind of train that goes up and down the hilly streets. Would you like to ride on one?

Circle the cable car in the photograph to the right.

Even though the Navajo people and the people in San Francisco both live with steep hills, their hills are very different!

UNIT **PROJECT** **Tip**

Work with your team to learn about the landforms in and around your community. Learn more about the climate in your community.

Australia

Koalas do not drink much water. They get water from the leaves they eat.

Australia is a big country. It is far away from the United States.

Look at the map below. What direction is the United States from Australia? About how far is Australia from the United States?

_____

Australia has many animals not found anywhere else. One of them is the small, furry koala. The koala lives in trees. Its food is the leaf of the eucalyptus tree. But many of these trees have disappeared.

Once, Australia had many thousands of koalas. Today, there are not quite as many. Some of them live in a special park in Brisbane. There, people take care of them. Many visitors come to see the koalas, too.

Look at the map. Find Brisbane. Circle it.

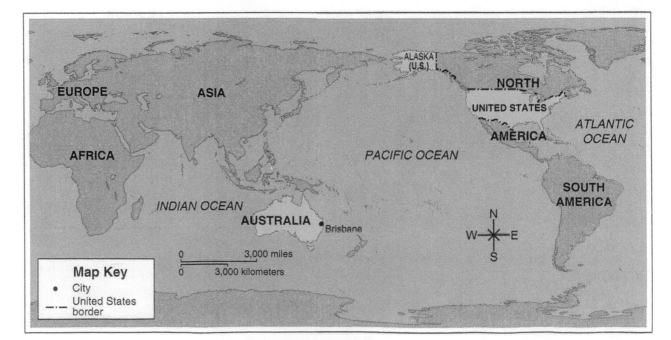

EUROPE
ASIA
ALASKA (U.S.)
NORTH
UNITED STATES
AMERICA
ATLANTIC OCEAN
AFRICA
PACIFIC OCEAN
INDIAN OCEAN
AUSTRALIA • Brisbane
SOUTH AMERICA

0   3,000 miles
0   3,000 kilometers

N
W—E
S

Map Key
• City
—··— United States border

CHAPTER ✓ CHECKUP

Finish each sentence. Circle the letter of the correct answer.

1. Two examples of a water resource are

   a. mountains and hills.
   b. lakes and rivers.
   c. oceans and plains.
   d. forests and climates.

2. Soil is an important resource for

   a. loggers.
   b. skiers.
   c. sailors.
   d. farmers.

3. Two mineral resources are

   a. gold and oil.
   b. sun and flowers.
   c. snow and gas.
   d. fish and rocks.

4. The weather over a period of time is called

   a. landform.
   b. valley.
   c. mineral.
   d. climate.

5. Most communities are found on

   a. hills.
   b. mountains.
   c. plains.
   d. rivers.

6. A landform that is low land between mountains is called a

   a. plain.
   b. valley.
   c. hill.
   d. canyon.

 Why do you think most communities are built on plains? What special problems might communities in mountains have?

_____

_____

_____

_____

Using a Landform Map

The map below shows the state of Arkansas. Use the map key to answer these questions.

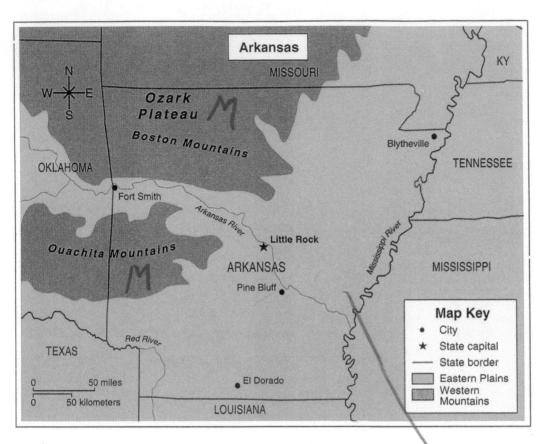

1. What are the two main kinds of landforms in Arkansas?

   Mountains

2. Find the picture on this page that shows plains. Draw a line from the picture of the plains to the plains shown on the map. Mark the mountains on the map with an <u>M</u>.

3. What is the capital of Arkansas?

   Little Rock

4. What does the land look like around Little Rock?

   Flat

Mountains

Plains

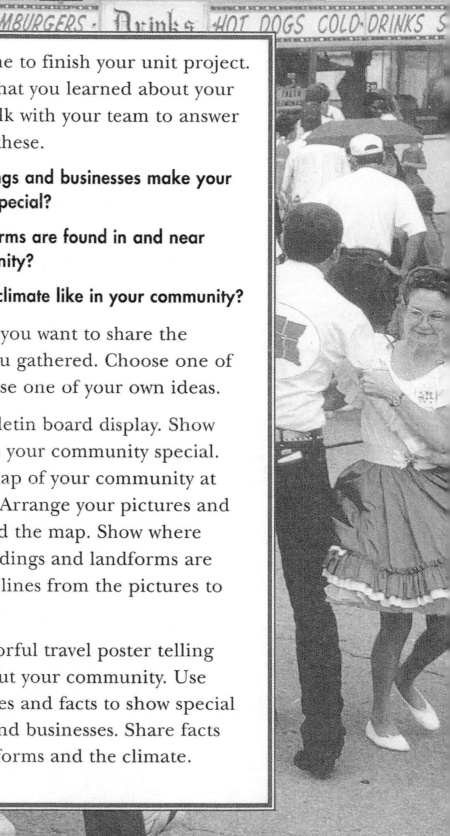

Now it is time to finish your unit project. Think about what you learned about your community. Talk with your team to answer questions like these.

- **What buildings and businesses make your community special?**

- **What landforms are found in and near your community?**

- **What is the climate like in your community?**

Decide how you want to share the information you gathered. Choose one of these ways or use one of your own ideas.

➤ Make a bulletin board display. Show what makes your community special. Put a big map of your community at the center. Arrange your pictures and facts around the map. Show where special buildings and landforms are by drawing lines from the pictures to the map.

➤ Make a colorful travel poster telling people about your community. Use your pictures and facts to show special buildings and businesses. Share facts about landforms and the climate.

UNIT 2

Kinds of Communities

Communities come in different sizes. Large communities are called cities. Thousands or even millions of people live in a city. Small communities are called towns. Towns have fewer people.

Unit 2 of this book will help you find answers to questions like these about different kinds of communities.

- What is life like in a city?
- What is life like in a town?

UNIT PROJECT

Start a team project. Learn about life in different kinds of communities so you can make travel brochures. Collect facts about communities. Collect pictures of them, too. Work on your project as you read Unit 2.

Small Communities

Do you live in a small community? If you do, you know one important thing about small communities. In small towns most people know one another.

Friends and Neighbors

People in small communities see one another a lot. They often shop in the same stores. They buy gas at the same station. They keep money in the same bank. Sometimes they work at the same kinds of jobs.

The picture below shows a small fishing town. People here like to go to the **docks** when the fishing boats come in. The docks are platforms built over the water. Boats load and unload at the docks.

Circle a dock in the photograph.

Many people in fishing towns depend on the sea.

It is easy to be friendly in a small town. People stop to say hello and to talk. They ask about friends, family, work, and other things. They tell each other the news.

Put a ✔ on a store shown in the photograph.

Circle something one of the people has just bought in a store.

Put an <u>X</u> on something in the picture that helps people get around their community.

It is easy to know lots of people in a small town.

The Langs sort fruits and vegetables by size and put them into boxes. The Langs also check them for bugs and rot.

Working in Small Communities

Many small towns are in **rural** areas. These are places in the country. These places are not cities.

The Lang family lives in Rose Hill, North Carolina. The **population** of Rose Hill is very small. Population is the number of people that live in a place.

Like their neighbors, the Langs are farmers. They raise turkeys, cattle, and hogs. They also grow peaches and sweet potatoes. The Langs need a lot of land for their animals and crops. They could not farm in a city.

Look at the photograph above. Circle what the Langs have grown. Think about their crops. Then explain why you cannot raise turkeys in the city. Write your answer here.

_____

_____

_____

Working Together

People in a small town work together to run their community. Many grown-ups may belong to the fire department. Whenever there is a fire, these people stop the work they are doing and rush to help. This is called a **volunteer** fire department. Volunteers are people who are not paid for the work they do.

People in a small community may also take their own garbage away. This way, the community does not have to pay workers to collect the garbage.

Why would a community use volunteer workers? Write your answer here.

_____

_____

_____

The fire departments of small, rural communities are often made up of volunteers.

UNIT PROJECT Tip

Gather facts about life in a small town. What do towns look like? What jobs do people do? Cut pictures of towns from magazines.

Some small towns in our country have amazing names! Have you ever heard of Sopchoppy or Moosup? They are both towns in the United States. Sopchoppy is in Florida. Moosup is in Connecticut.

These towns aren't the only ones with unusual names. Some people in Idaho live in a community called Chubbuck. Shinglehouse is a small town in Pennsylvania. Rocky Boy, Montana, is another small town.

Look at the map. Circle these communities: Sugar Land, Paw Paw, and Winter.

Find two more communities with unusual names on the map. Write the names here.

_____

_____

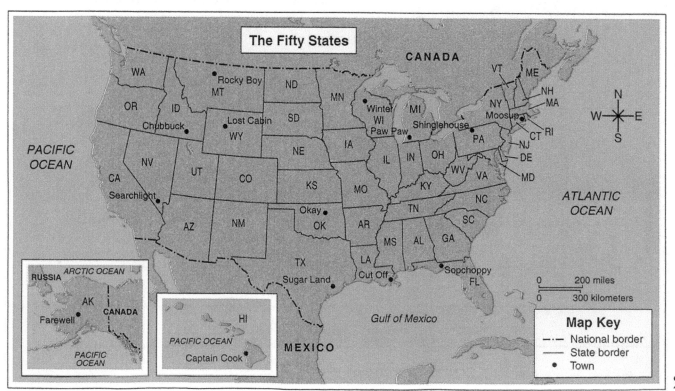

29

CHAPTER ✓ CHECKUP

Finish each sentence. Circle the letter of the correct answer.

1. Small communities are called

   a. cities.

   b. rural.

   c. states.

   d. towns.

2. Most people in small communities

   a. do not know each other.

   b. do not greet one another.

   c. often see each other.

   d. often act unfriendly.

3. An area in the country is called

   a. a rural area.

   b. a town dump.

   c. a wildlife area.

   d. an office building.

4. Population is

   a. the number of people who are friendly.

   b. how long it takes to get to a city.

   c. another name for a small community.

   d. the number of people who live in a place.

5. People in small communities

   a. live near lots of tall buildings.

   b. do not have room to farm.

   c. sometimes take away their own garbage.

   d. never shop in the same stores.

6. People in communities can help by

   a. going skiing.

   b. being volunteers.

   c. getting training.

   d. being farmers.

 Imagine you are writing to a friend about life in a small town. Explain why life in your small town is friendly. Write your answer here.

_____

_____

_____

Suburban Communities

Lots of Americans live in **suburbs.** A suburb is a community near a big city. Some suburbs can be cities themselves. But suburbs are always near a larger city.

Living in a Suburb

The picture shows Forest Park, Georgia. It is a suburb near Atlanta. The Wilsons live here. Most suburbs have homes like the ones in Forest Park. The houses and apartment buildings have yards. Many homes have garages and driveways.

Like many people who live in suburbs, Mrs. Wilson works in the city nearby. She works at the Atlanta airport.

Look at the photograph. How is this suburb different from a small community? Write your answer here.

_____

Most suburbs are quiet and peaceful. Stores and shops are usually a short drive away.

31

There are many reasons why the Wilsons like Forest Park. They think the big city is too crowded and noisy. In Forest Park the streets are quiet. There's a shopping center nearby. But the Wilsons like being near the city, too. They can work and have fun in Atlanta.

There are more reasons why the Wilsons like Forest Park. The suburb is close to the city, but it feels like a small town. The family has lots of friends and neighbors who live in the community. The Wilsons like the schools, too. Both Beth and John Wilson walk to a school in their own neighborhood. And there's enough room for Mrs. Wilson's garden!

Look at the picture. Find two things the Wilsons like about suburbs. Write your answer here.

_____

_____

People in suburbs take care of their yards. Sometimes that means a lot of work!

32

A system of roads called expressways are used for traveling between suburbs and cities.

Getting Around in Suburbs

In suburbs a lot of land is used for homes. Land is also used for roads. It can be a long way from one end of a suburb to another! So people who live in suburbs need to use **transportation.** Transportation is how people or things get from place to place. Most people in suburbs use cars for transportation.

Many people drive to work. Mrs. Wilson drives from Forest Park to Atlanta. People also need cars to go shopping, to visit the doctor, or to go to the movies.

Circle a form of transportation shown in the photograph.

UNIT PROJECT Tip

Gather facts and pictures about life in suburbs. How do suburbs look? Where do people work and play? Is your community like a suburb?

The Oliveras enjoy their home in Union City.

The Olivera family lives in Union City. It is a suburb of San Francisco, California. The Oliveras live there because it is quieter than San Francisco. In Union City the Oliveras can afford to own a house.

When the Oliveras go to San Francisco, they take trains. The trains link San Francisco with the communities around it. Trains link many suburbs to nearby cities.

 Find the compass rose on the map below. The long lines on the compass rose show the main directions. The four short lines stand for in-between directions. For example, the direction between north and east is northeast.

Find San Francisco on the map. Then find Union City. Draw a line from San Francisco to Union City.

Draw a line under the name of a community southwest of Union City.

Put a ✔ in front of the name of a community northwest of Union City.

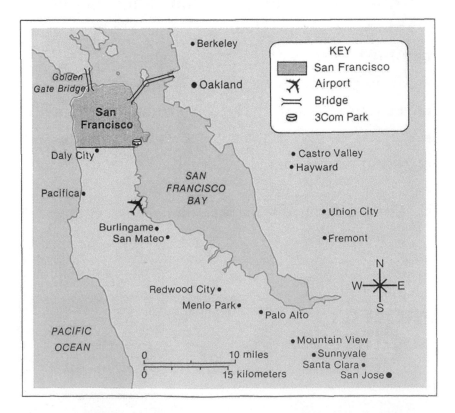

The BART trains the Oliveras take in Union City run above ground. But when those trains get to San Francisco, they run underground. Underground trains are called subways. When the traffic is stuck above ground, the trains are still moving along underground. So sometimes it is a good idea to leave your car behind. You might get where you're going faster in the subway!

The first subway in the United States was built in Boston, Massachusetts, in 1897. It was only one-and-a-half miles long when it opened. But it has grown since then!

Now, many subways connect suburbs and cities. Have you ever ridden on one?

Why do people travel on the subway? Write your answer here.

_____

This photograph of a Boston subway station was taken in 1898.

CHAPTER ✓ CHECKUP

Finish each sentence. Circle the letter of the correct answer.

1. A suburb is a
   a. small fishing village.
   b. community outside a city.
   c. kind of shopping center.
   d. rural community.

2. Many people in suburbs work
   a. in nearby cities.
   b. at cutting down trees.
   c. at busy airports.
   d. in Union City.

3. The land in suburbs is used mostly for
   a. offices and trains.
   b. camping and hiking.
   c. roads and houses.
   d. farms and gardens.

4. The way people get from one place to another is called
   a. fishing.
   b. transportation.
   c. suburbs.
   d. maps.

5. Most people get from place to place in suburbs by
   a. bus.
   b. train.
   c. plane.
   d. car.

6. Trains that travel underground are called
   a. cable cars.
   b. tunnels.
   c. suburbs.
   d. subways.

THINKING AND WRITING Why do some people like suburbs better than small towns?

_____

_____

_____

_____

_____

CHAPTER 5

Cities

What makes a city different from a town? Its size, that's what! A city is much bigger than a town. Many people live and work in cities.

Cities Are Big

The photograph shows the city of Los Angeles, California. Nearly 4 million people live there. There are many very tall buildings in Los Angeles. People work in some of those buildings. Families live in tall buildings, too. There just isn't enough room for everyone to have houses. So, many people in cities live in apartments in tall buildings. All communities have buildings, but cities have many more.

Put a ✔ by something in the photograph you cannot see in a rural community.

With its skyscrapers, offices, and homes, Los Angeles covers a lot of land.

Most cities have an area that is used mostly for business. This area is often called "downtown." People go downtown to work in big office buildings and to shop.

Look at the map of downtown Danville below. Find the area of the city near the ocean. Cities by the water often have a **harbor**. A harbor is a safe place for ships. There, big ships load and unload.

 Put an X on the part of the map that shows the harbor.

What direction would you travel to get from the stores on Park Lane to the bridge over Cantwell River?

_____

The ships take things made in the city to other communities. They also bring food and other things to the city. In cities a lot of buildings cover the land. So there is no room to grow food.

Trace the shortest route from the warehouses on Water Street to the Bruce Street Apartments.

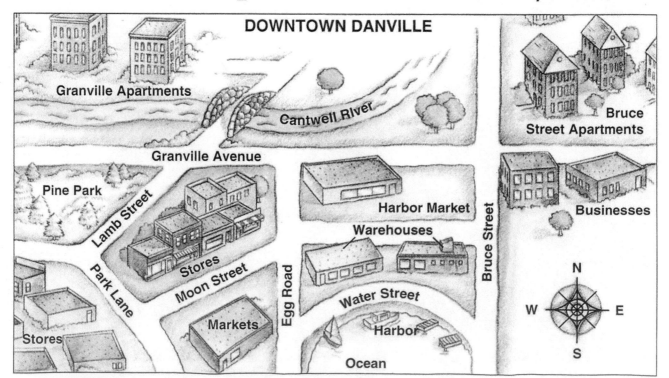

DOWNTOWN DANVILLE

Granville Apartments

Cantwell River

Bruce Street Apartments

Granville Avenue

Pine Park

Lamb Street

Harbor Market

Businesses

Warehouses

Bruce Street

Stores

Moon Street

Egg Road

Water Street

N

W   E

S

Markets

Harbor

Stores

Ocean

Working in Cities

People in cities work at many different kinds of jobs. Some people sell things in stores. Others unload the ships that come into the harbor. Still others write books or work on newspapers. Do you like to watch television? People who work for television usually work in cities, too.

Many cities have buildings called **factories** where things are made. Things made by people are called **goods.** Toys, pencils, and washing machines are all goods that people make in factories. Can you think of other goods that people make? Chances are they are made in a city.

■ **Circle what is being made in the photograph.**

It takes many people working together to make goods in factories.

39

Living in a City

The Kwan family lives in Austin, Texas. Austin is the capital of Texas. Mr. and Mrs. Kwan both work in the city.

The whole family likes to have fun in Austin. Like most cities, Austin has many things to do. The Kwans can go places to hear music. They can see plays and movies.

The family can even watch a football game. Do you have a favorite team? Many cities have sports teams.

Cities also have parks. At a city park, you can have a picnic, ride your bike, play volleyball, or take a walk.

Name one way the Kwans can have fun in Austin. Write your answer here.

_____

(above) The Kwan family enjoys being together outside. (below, right) The Kwan family sometimes visits the State Capitol building in Austin.

UNIT **PROJECT** Tip

Collect facts and pictures about city life. What do cities look like? Where do people live, work, and play? Are cities like your community?

40

Toronto is a big city in Canada. Canada is the country north of the United States.

Toronto is like some cities in the United States. It has a downtown with tall, modern buildings. Most of these buildings are banks, offices, and stores. Toronto also has parks and a zoo.

Many people in Toronto work in factories. Clothes and paper are made in Toronto.

Toronto has a subway. Toronto is also a big transportation center in Canada. Many ships sail from its harbor. People and goods also arrive in Toronto by train and by airplane.

Name two ways Toronto is like some big cities in the United States. Write your answer here.

_____

_____

Toronto, Canada, has many tall, modern buildings.

41

CHAPTER ✓ CHECKUP

Finish each sentence. Circle the letter of the correct answer.

1. Many people in cities live in
   a. factories.
   b. museums.
   c. farmhouses.
   d. apartments.

2. The downtown part of a city is mostly
   a. for business.
   b. for living.
   c. for airports.
   d. for parks.

3. In cities the land is used mainly for
   a. farming.
   b. subways.
   c. buildings.
   d. suburbs.

4. When ships come to cities, they unload at a
   a. factory.
   b. subway.
   c. park.
   d. harbor.

5. Buildings where things are made are called
   a. apartments.
   b. subways.
   c. factories.
   d. harbors.

6. Two goods made in factories are
   a. fish and trees.
   b. toys and cars.
   c. turkeys and pigs.
   d. clothes and cats.

 THINKING AND WRITING Imagine you live in a big city. Tell why you think the city is special and exciting. Write your answer here.

_____

_____

_____

_____

_____

Your Own Community

You have read about three kinds of communities. In this chapter you will look at the community where you live.

Different Places

The pictures below show how the land is used in different kinds of communities.

Look at the pictures. Put a ✔ under the picture that shows a city.

Put an X under the picture that shows a small town.

Draw a line under the picture that shows a suburb.

Circle the community that is most like the place where you live.

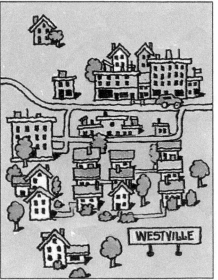

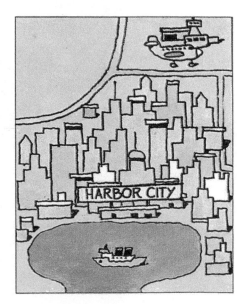

Your **address** tells where you live.

 Write your name and address here.

_____

_____

_____

A **political map** can tell where you live, too. This one of the United States shows states and their **borders.** A border is a line that shows where one place ends and another place begins.

Find your state on the map. Circle it.

Mexico is the country south of the United States. Write the name of a state that is on the border of Mexico.

_____

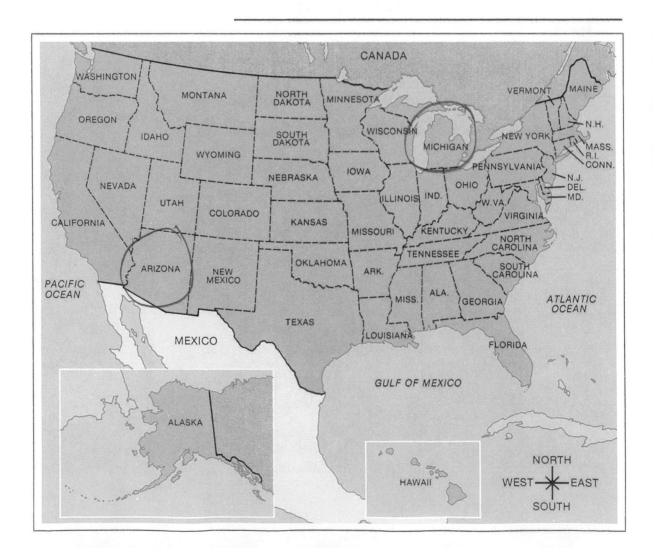

Finding Out

It does not matter whether your community is large or small. There are still many things to learn about it.

What do you know about your community? What would you like to know? Here is a list of questions that one class made.

1. What are some special places to visit?

2. What natural resources do we have?

3. What goods do we make? What crops do we grow?

4. Who is our community proud of?

5. How can we help our community?

Think of a question of your own to write here.

_____

_____

New York City has more people than any other community in our nation. There are many places to visit in New York City.

(right) Most communities have people who build and fix houses. Perhaps someone in your family does this kind of work. (below) In the library you can learn all kinds of things about your community.

Start to find out about your community by asking questions. Talk to people who work in your community. Begin with your family. Find out about their jobs. Do they make things? Do they sell things? Do people in your family grow things or help others? Do they work for pay or do they volunteer?

To learn more about your community, you will need to do some hunting. A good place to look is the public library. Take a list of questions with you.

 To begin your list, write a question here.

_____

Take a notebook, too. You may find books in the library about your state and about your community. If you don't, or if you need help, you can ask a librarian.

In the 1890s, many people came to Skagway, Alaska, because gold had been discovered nearby.

Old pictures can tell you about the past, too. You can find plenty of pictures at the library. This picture shows what Skagway, Alaska, looked like many years ago. Your community probably looked very different at one time, too!

Look at the picture. Circle one kind of transportation that people used in the past.

How can you tell this photograph is old? Write your answer here.

_____

_____

UNIT PROJECT Tip As you work on your project, ask questions like those found on page 45.

Phillis Wheatley

When Phillis Wheatley was 14 years old, she did something special. She started to write poetry. That was in the year 1767.

Phillis was an African American. At that time most African Americans were not allowed to learn to read or write. Most African Americans were **slaves.** A slave is a person who is owned by another person. Phillis was a slave, too. She was brought to Boston on a slave ship when she was eight. The people who owned Phillis taught her to read and write. They were very happy when she started to write her poems.

In 1773 Phillis had her first book of poems printed. She became our first African American poet.

Phillis Wheatley later became free. She married John Peters who had also once been a slave.

Phillis Wheatley wrote poems about things she cared about. What would you write a poem about? Write your answer here.

_____

_____

_____

CHAPTER ✓ CHECKUP

Complete each sentence. Circle the letter of the correct answer.

1. Three kinds of communities are
   a. towns, cities, and subways.
   b. rural, towns, and suburbs.
   c. towns, suburbs, and cities.
   d. cities, streets, and countries.

2. A political map helps you
   a. do your work.
   b. find out where places are.
   c. learn to add and subtract.
   d. look up books.

3. On a map you can tell where a state ends because of its
   a. borders.
   b. oceans.
   c. resources.
   d. crops.

4. You can find facts about your community
   a. in a hospital.
   b. in the public library.
   c. in a city.
   d. from a sports team.

5. Another way to learn about your community is to
   a. play ball.
   b. go shopping.
   c. go on a long trip.
   d. ask people questions.

6. You can learn about life long ago through
   a. your address.
   b. old pictures.
   c. new buildings.
   d. new pictures.

 THINKING AND WRITING Is your community a small town, a suburb, or a city? Explain your choice. Write your answer here.

_____

_____

_____

_____

_____

Unit 2 Skill Builder

Reading a Political Map

You know that the United States is made up of 50 states. The map below is a political map of Alaska. Alaska is the biggest state in the United States.

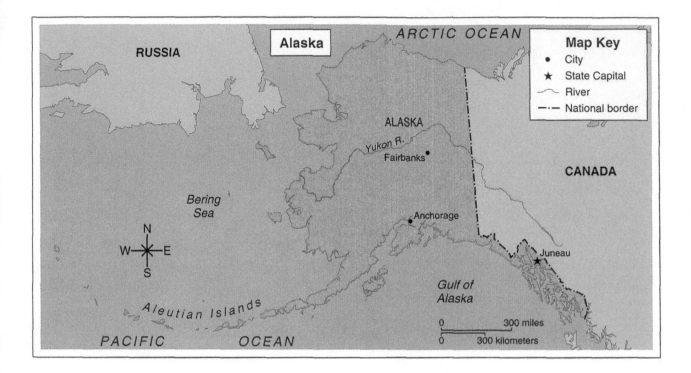

1. Look at the map key. Circle the symbol for rivers.

2. Find a river on the map. Trace the path of the river to the ocean.

3. Look at the map key again. Find the symbol for state capital. Circle Alaska's capital.

4. What ocean is northeast of Alaska?

   _____

5. Find the symbol for national borders. Then find a national border on the map. What nation's border is it? Write your answer here.

   _____

Now it is time to finish your unit project. Think about what you learned about different kinds of communities.

- **What is life like in a small town?**
- **What is life like in a city?**
- **What is life like in a suburb?**
- **Is your community a town, suburb, or city?**

Decide how you want to share the information you gathered. Choose one of these ways or use one of your own ideas.

➤ Have your team choose either a small town, a suburb, or a city. Make a travel brochure about your kind of community. Give your community a name. Explain what life is like there in words and pictures. Share information about kinds of work and play. You might want to make a few postcards to include in your brochure.

➤ Make a large mural of your team's community. Show how it is a town, suburb, or city.

➤ Use your facts and pictures to make a book on communities.

➤ Draw a map of the kind of community your team studied. Label it as a town, suburb, or city. Make a display of facts and pictures about life in this kind of community.

UNIT 3

People Work in Communities

People in communities work at many jobs. Often people work together to make things. The things that workers make and do are useful to other people. Some of these things are probably useful to you!

Unit 3 of this book will help you find answers to questions like these about people and their work.

- Why do communities need workers?

- How do communities make life easier for workers?

PROJECT

Start a team project. Collect facts about the kind of workers who provide the things you need. You can use the facts to show how workers make things. Work on your project as you read Unit 3.

Meeting Needs and Wants

This morning you woke up and put on your clothes. Clothes are things that everyone needs. Then you had breakfast. People also need food to live. You did all of this in your home. Everyone needs a place to live. This place is called **shelter.** Food, clothes, and shelter are **needs** for everyone in a community. Needs are things you must have in order to live.

Why People Work

People work to meet their needs. They use the money they earn to buy what they need.

People also use money to buy their **wants.** Wants are things you would like to have. You don't need these things to live.

The man in the photograph below is buying plants for his home. Is a plant a want or a need? Write *want* or *need* here.

_____

The man uses the money he makes to pay for things he needs and wants.

53

Look at the pictures below. In the first picture, the boy is making something.

■ **Circle the tool the boy is using.**

In the second picture, the boy is selling what he has made. A person who grows or makes things for sale is a **producer.**

■ **Show that the boy is a producer. Write *producer* below the second picture.**

Now look at the third picture. How is the boy spending his money? When people make money, they can spend it for something that they want or need. A person who buys something to eat or to use is a **consumer.**

■ **Show that the boy is a consumer. Write *consumer* below the third picture.**

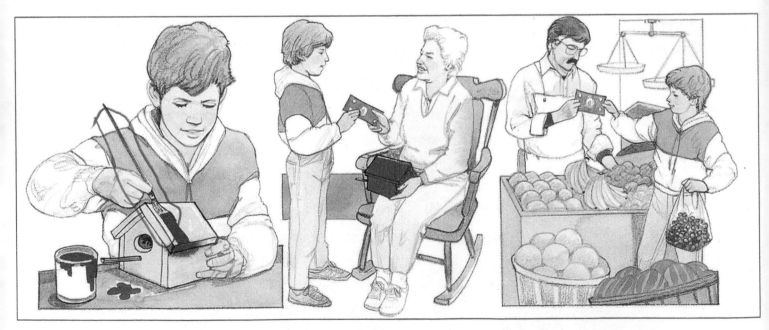

Talk with your team about what it means to be a consumer. Make a list of things that you and your team members buy.

People Need Services

Do you take your clothes to a cleaner? Have you ever been to the dentist for a checkup? Who do you visit to get your hair cut?

If you have done any of these things, you have used a **service.** A service is something people do that other people need or want.

Services are one reason people live together in communities. Different people can do different work. If you lived all by yourself, you would have to do everything yourself. You would not have time for anything else.

Look at the picture below. The girl is getting a checkup.

Circle the person who is giving the service.

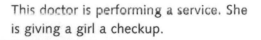

This doctor is performing a service. She is giving a girl a checkup.

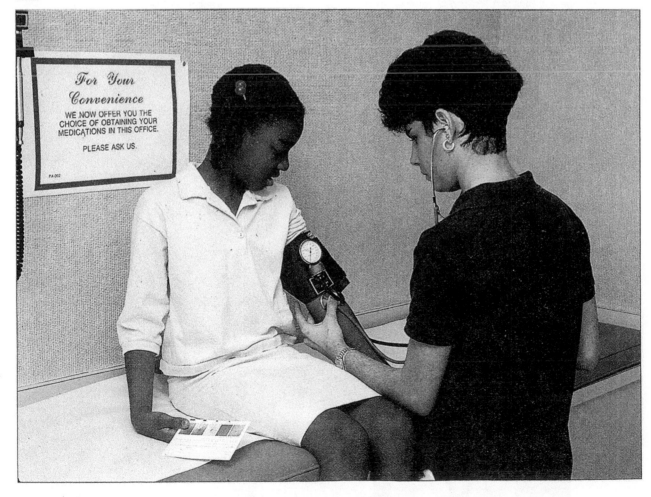

Look at the picture below. The man is checking the community's water to make sure it is safe to drink. This is a service that communities provide. Later you will learn more about other services that communities offer.

People who work for the community make money for doing their jobs. They use the money they earn to buy food, clothes, and other things.

Why is it important for a community to have clean water? Write your answer here.

_____

_____

Workers make sure that the water is safe for the community.

Today, more people than ever work in service jobs. In 1900, almost one out of every two people farmed. Now, most people have service jobs. More than twice as many people have this kind of job as any other kind.

People who repair computers or shoes or cars are service workers. So are nurses, teachers, and lawyers. Service workers are also the people who run hotels and work in television and the movies. Think about the people you know. How many of them are service workers?

Look at the pictures below. Label the producer. Circle what the person is producing.

Write an X on the service worker.

(left) This woman is watering plants that are for sale. (right) This man climbs a ladder to paint the house.

Come to the street fair!

Look at the picture below. Circle two people who are service workers.

Put an **X** on three consumers.

What are two things you can buy at this fair? Write your answer here.

_____

Jane Addams

Sometimes people do not have enough money to pay for their needs and wants. Jane Addams saw many people like this. She wanted to do something to help them.

Jane Addams lived in Chicago over 100 years ago. As a young woman, she moved to a poor part of the city. Many people who lived there had just come to the United States. Jane started Hull House in this area in 1889. Hull House was a special community center. Jane worked to make community life better.

Jane Addams

At Hull House, people from other countries learned to speak English. Parents could leave children there while they went to work. At Hull House, people could join reading groups and a music school. Hull House also had doctors and nurses.

People in other communities heard about Jane Addams's work. They wanted to help needy people in their cities, too. Soon other communities had places like Hull House.

Today, Hull House has six centers in Chicago and 35 in the Chicago area. These centers offer people the same kind of help Jane Addams did 100 years ago.

Why would a place like Hull House be important for people who have just come to a community? Write your answer here.

_____

_____

CHAPTER ✓ CHECKUP

Finish each sentence. Circle the letter of the correct answer.

1. Three needs people have are
   a. food, shelter, clothes.
   b. services, toys, homes.
   c. movies, money, fairs.
   d. barbers, records, cleaners.

2. A want is something
   a. you need to live.
   b. you make yourself.
   c. you do not need to live.
   d. producers use to make things.

3. A producer is someone who
   a. pays for things.
   b. uses things.
   c. makes things.
   d. needs things.

4. When you buy something to eat, you are a
   a. teacher.
   b. consumer.
   c. builder.
   d. producer.

5. When you go to a dentist, you are
   a. doing a job.
   b. getting a haircut.
   c. working for money.
   d. using a service.

6. Workers pay for their needs with
   a. tickets.
   b. money.
   c. doctors.
   d. shelter.

THINKING AND WRITING

Write about one of your wants. Explain why it is a want and not a need.

_____

_____

_____

_____

_____

_____

Communities Need One Another

What did you wear to school today? Your clothes might have come from a store in your community. But they were probably made somewhere else. No community makes and grows everything it needs.

Goods from Many Communities

The things you need and want come from many different communities. (Remember that things that are made by people are called goods.) Some goods arrive by airplane. Others arrive by train. How many different kinds of cars do you see on this train? Each one carries something different. Maybe this train is headed for your community.

How else can goods get to your community? Write your answer here.

_____

People in communities buy and sell goods made in other places. Some goods are carried by train.

61

Making Bread

Have you ever made bread? If so, you know there are many steps in making it. A **flow chart** shows the step-by-step order in which something is done. This flow chart shows all the steps in making bread. It takes many people in many communities to make the bread you buy in a store. Read each step. Then follow the arrow to the next step.

How to Make Bread

1. A farmer plants the seeds to grow wheat.

 Put an X on two natural resources that help the farmer grow wheat.

2. When the wheat is ready, it is cut.

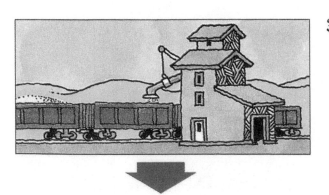

3. The wheat goes by truck to a grain elevator. From the elevator, the wheat goes to a mill by train.

Circle the wheat going from the elevator to the train.

4. Workers in the mill wash, dry, and crush the wheat. Then they make it into flour.

Circle the bags of flour that come from the mill.

5. Next, the flour goes from the mill to the bakery.

What kind of transportation is used? Write your answer here.

_____

6. Bakers make dough from the flour and bake the bread in hot ovens. Mmmm! Then the bread is sliced and wrapped.

7. Now the bread is on its way to other communities.

Circle the place where the driver takes the bread.

8. The bread goes onto shelves.

What happens next? Write your answer here.

_____

Circle two people who work in the store.

A Chain of Workers

Many workers help get bread to your community. It takes many workers to get most things to your stores. The workers form a kind of chain. If workers in one community do not do their jobs, the chain breaks.

> Look at the flow chart below. Put a ✔ under the first worker in the chain.
>
> Put an X under the worker who makes sure the milk is heated.
>
> Circle the worker who delivers the milk.

People depend on other workers for their jobs. If the farmer doesn't milk the cows, then the other workers cannot do their jobs.

How to Make Chocolate Milk

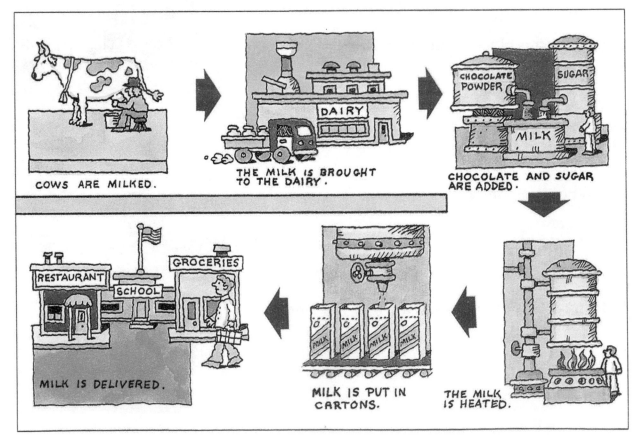

COWS ARE MILKED.

THE MILK IS BROUGHT TO THE DAIRY.

CHOCOLATE AND SUGAR ARE ADDED.

MILK IS DELIVERED.

MILK IS PUT IN CARTONS.

THE MILK IS HEATED.

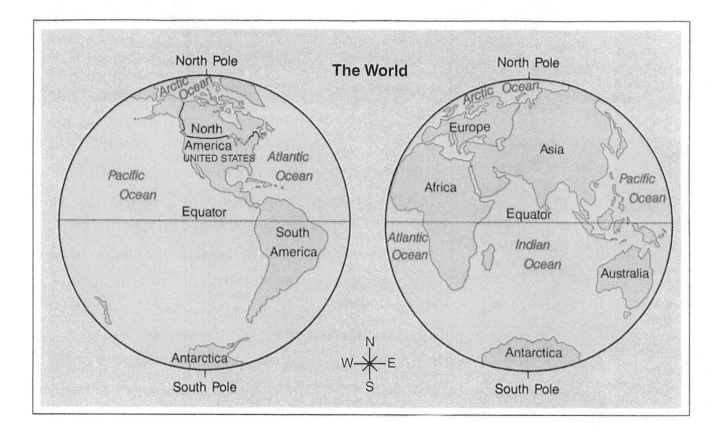

The World

Countries Can Help Each Other

Few countries make all the things they need and want. Some nations in Asia can't grow enough food for all their needs. They buy wheat from other nations, like the United States. This is one way that communities around the world help one another.

Look at the pictures of a **globe.** A globe is a model of Earth. The pictures are flat, so you can see just one side of the globe at a time.

Circle the United States on the left globe.

Put an X on the part of the globe that shows the continent of Asia.

UNIT PROJECT Tip

Look at the list of items your team made. Next to each item list the workers you think helped make and deliver the items. Then check an encyclopedia to see if you were right!

Market Women

Market women have to be good at business. They use the money they make to pay for their needs and wants.

Most of the things you buy come from stores. But if you lived in the city of Onitsha, you might not go to stores. You might go to the market instead. Onitsha is in Nigeria, a country in Africa. The Onitsha market is one of the biggest in the world. It is very famous.

Many Nigerian women sell their goods in Onitsha's market. What can you buy from them? You can buy just about anything. Food, clothes, soap, radios, rugs, chairs, and even parts for a car are all for sale.

Look at the pictures. Circle two containers the women use to hold the food they sell.

How do these market women depend on farmers? Write your answer here.

_____

_____

CHAPTER ✔ CHECKUP

Finish each sentence. Circle the letter in front of the correct answer.

1. Two important ways goods are carried to communities are by

   a. bicycle and boat.
   b. train and airplane.
   c. car and cart.
   d. tractor and bus.

2. A flow chart shows

   a. how a train travels.
   b. the step-by-step order in which something is done.
   c. the way farmers cut wheat.
   d. how to find countries on a map.

3. The first step in making bread is done by a

   a. baker.
   b. seller.
   c. miller.
   d. farmer.

4. At a mill, wheat is made into

   a. bread.
   b. grain.
   c. flour.
   d. money.

5. If people in one community do not do their jobs, the chain of workers

   a. grows.
   b. breaks.
   c. bakes.
   d. buys.

6. You can look at a globe to find out

   a. how much bread costs.
   b. where milk comes from.
   c. where Asia is in the world.
   d. how to get to school.

 Would you rather be a producer or a service worker? Tell what product you would like to produce or what service you would offer. Explain your reason.

_____

_____

_____

_____

Unit 3 Skill Builder
Using a Flow Chart

As you know, producers can make goods or services. The flow chart below shows you how producers meet consumers' wants and needs.

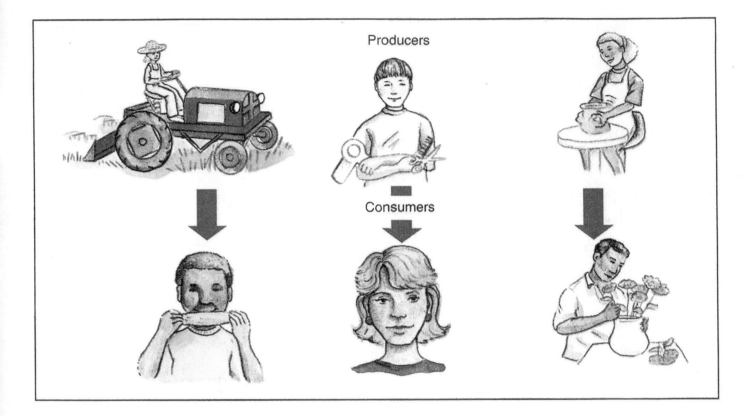

1. Circle the producer who is a service worker.

2. Underline the consumer who bought something that is a need.

3. Which consumer bought a service? Write your answer here.

_____

4. Did the consumer who bought a service meet a need or a want? Explain your answer.

_____

_____

Now it's time to finish your unit project. Think about what you learned about producers and consumers. Talk with your team about questions like these.

- **What do consumers do?**

- **How do producers make items you buy?**

Decide how you want to show the information you gathered. Choose one of these ways or use one of your own ideas.

➤ Go over your list of items and the workers who make them. Choose the best examples and draw pictures of them. Then use your pictures to make a flow chart to show how your product reaches the consumer.

➤ Make a "How To" booklet. Work with your team to make a booklet that shows each of the steps in making one of the items your team learned about.

UNIT 4

Who Runs Our Communities?

Every community needs to make decisions about building schools, putting up street signs, and making laws. You will find out how people in different communities decide about these things.

Unit 4 of this book will help you find answers to questions like these about how communities work.

- Who runs a community?
- Why do communities have laws?
- How do communities provide services?

UNIT PROJECT

Start a team project. Form a student planning team. Gather information about things your school needs. You will use the facts to hold an election. Work on your project as you read Unit 4.

LLY R. McDANIEL
MAYOR—PLACE I

FLOYD T. HAR
CITY MANAGER

Communities Have a Government

Have you ever played the game Follow the Leader? If so, you know that the leader is the person who decides what you will do.

A community has leaders, too. These leaders help a community make important choices.

Choosing Leaders

People in communities have many different jobs. Some are doctors or teachers. Others are bankers or shopkeepers.

However, each member of a community has to help make choices for the community, too. One way people do this is by voting for leaders to run the community. Voting is a fair way for people to choose their leaders.

Look at the picture. Circle the American flag at this community meeting.

These people have been chosen by the voters to run their community.

71

Before people vote, they think carefully. They think about the people running for office. Will their ideas be good for the community? Will their ideas be good for me?

Look at the picture. Underline the words that tell what the speaker promises to do.

When you are older, you will vote for community leaders. Now, you can vote for class leaders. Ms. Carter's students voted for a class leader. You can see the results on the **bar graph.** A bar graph uses bars to stand for numbers. It helps you compare different groups of numbers.

VOTES FOR CLASS LEADER

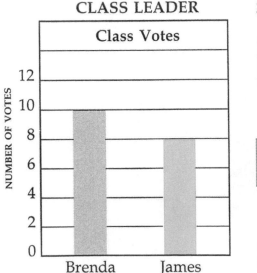

Read the title and the words at the bottom of each bar. What do the bars show?

_____

Read the words on the left side of the graph. What do the numbers stand for?

_____

Write the number of votes next to each name. Circle the winner's name.

Brenda _____   James _____

A Look at Leaders

The leaders who make choices and rules for a community are part of its **government.** A community has three main kinds of leaders in its government. Let's see who they are.

The **lawmakers** make new **laws** or change old ones. Rules for communities are called laws.

The **mayor** is the main leader of the government in many communities. One of the mayor's jobs is to make sure the community's laws are obeyed. Does your community have a mayor?

A **judge** decides if a law has been broken. The place where judges work is a court.

Look at the pictures. Number the lawmakers *1,* the mayor *2,* and the judge *3.*

UNIT PROJECT Tip

With your team, discuss things at your school that you want to improve. Think about the playground, classrooms, gym, or computers.

Government Leaders at Work

A mayor tries to solve problems in a community. The mayor works with lawmakers to pass laws that will improve things.

A mayor also tries to make sure that the people in a community get all the services they need. A mayor chooses other people to help provide these services. Can you name the chief of police in your community? The mayor probably chose this person for the job. Look at the **chart** below. A chart presents facts in a way that is easy to read.

> **Circle the person who makes sure that community health laws are not broken.**

The leaders of a community want to make it a good place to live. So they try to be sure that the people in a community follow its laws. Judges decide what to do with people who break the laws.

People Chosen by Mayor	Their Jobs
Fire Chief:	runs the fire department
Police Chief:	runs the police department
Health Inspector:	makes sure that community health laws are not broken
Consumer Protector:	makes sure that laws protecting buyers and sellers are not broken
Building Inspector:	makes sure that buildings meet safety laws

One of our country's most famous leaders was Thomas Jefferson. He was born in 1743, over 250 years ago. At that time, our country was ruled by Great Britain, a country on the other side of the Atlantic Ocean.

Jefferson was a good student. Each day he spent about 15 hours reading and studying. In time, he became a lawmaker in Virginia.

Jefferson began his life's work in the late 1700s. At that time, many Americans were unhappy with British rule. They wanted to break away and start a new nation. They were willing to fight for their freedom.

Thomas Jefferson

Jefferson agreed with these ideas. He wrote a statement that expressed what many Americans felt. This statement is called the Declaration of Independence. It explained why America should be free. Even today, when people talk about freedom, they sometimes use the words of Thomas Jefferson.

Jefferson's role as a leader did not stop after he wrote the Declaration of Independence. He served the government of the United States in many ways. He is best known as our country's third President. Today he is still one of the most famous leaders in American history.

What is one thing Thomas Jefferson did for the United States? Write your answer here.

_____

CHAPTER ✓ CHECKUP

Finish each sentence. Circle the letter of the correct answer.

1. An important job of a community leader is to

    a. break laws.
    b. play games.
    c. make promises.
    d. make choices.

2. Communities choose leaders by

    a. thinking.
    b. building.
    c. voting.
    d. writing.

3. Two community leaders people vote for are

    a. mayor and lawmaker.
    b. doctor and shopkeeper.
    c. artist and judge.
    d. banker and teacher.

4. One of the mayor's jobs is to

    a. decide if a law has been broken.
    b. make new laws.
    c. run the fire department.
    d. provide community services.

5. Judges are community leaders who

    a. make new laws.
    b. see that laws are obeyed.
    c. provide community services.
    d. decide if laws are broken.

6. The main reason new laws are passed in a community is to

    a. help the police.
    b. improve things.
    c. punish people.
    d. keep courts busy.

Why do communities need leaders? Write your answer here.

_____

_____

_____

_____

_____

Communities Have Rules and Laws

Have you ever played checkers? Can you name some rules in checkers? Rules help people make choices. Rules tell us what to do or not to do. Rules tell us what is fair, too.

Look at the picture. Put an X on the girl who is taking her turn.

Using Rules

Most families have rules. Schools have rules, too. Do you say "thank you" when someone gives you a gift? Many rules are about being polite and kind. You may have learned them from your family, friends, or teachers.

Other rules help keep people safe and healthy. Do you have a rule about no running in your school halls? That rule is for safety.

Rules make a game more fun. What happens when someone doesn't follow the rules?

Breaking rules can cause all kinds of problems. Let's see what some might be.

Put an <u>X</u> on the girl who broke a rule about homework.

Circle the girl who did not follow a softball rule.

What rule did the boy break when he dropped paper on the playground? Write the rule here.

_____

Rules for Communities

Rules for communities are called laws. You read in Chapter 9 about some of the leaders who make and help keep the laws.

Communities have laws for the same reasons that families, schools, and games have rules. Laws help people make good choices about what is fair. Laws also help the people of a community live and work together.

The signs on this page show some laws in a community.

Circle the sign that tells people how fast they can drive their cars.

Find the sign that tells about a law near a school. Look at the words on the sign and write them on the line below.

_____

Look at the traffic light. Draw an arrow that points to the color that means "GO."

PROJECT Tip Meet with your team of student planners. Brainstorm a list of rules you think would make school better for everyone. Write down all of your ideas. Then pick the top three.

Laws at Work

Mrs. French is getting a ticket. She drove faster than the speed limit allows. Now she will have to pay a fine.

Look at the picture. Circle the sign that tells how fast Mrs. French can drive.

Look at the picture again. Why do you think the speed limit is so low? Write your answer here.

_____

If Mrs. French thinks she was not wrong, she can go to traffic court. A judge will hear her side of the story. The judge will decide whether or not Mrs. French has broken the law.

Communities have many laws about cars and traffic.

80

A community has many laws to protect people's health, too. Did you know there are laws that make sure buildings are safe?

Most communities have laws about food and restaurants. By law, every restaurant has to be clean. Inspectors visit every restaurant in the community. They make sure the kitchens are scrubbed clean every day. They check to be sure the food is kept fresh and cold, too.

Look at the picture below. Put an X on the inspector.

What is the other worker doing? Write your answer here.

_____

Did you go to the doctor for a checkup before you started school this year? Getting a checkup is a law in many communities. This law makes sure that students get the shots they need to stay healthy. Why would it be unfair to others if you did not obey this law?

When restaurants do not follow the law, they have to pay a fine. Sometimes they are closed.

81

How many people live in your community? One way to find out is to read a **census** report. A census is a count of how many people live in a place. Government census workers find out how many people live in each community in the nation.

Every ten years since 1790 the United States government has taken a census. Government workers used to do all the adding of numbers without the help of computers. Today people fill out special forms that can be read by a computer. The computer does the adding much more quickly than people can!

The census report is important to communities. It helps government leaders decide what kinds of services a community needs. Does a city need more schools? Does a town need highways to link it to other communities? Facts in the census report can help leaders make choices.

 Look at the map on the left. Circle the area that shows where the most people live.

Boone County
Missouri

Housing Units
Per Square Mile

OVER 500

(above) This census map gives information about where people live. (right) A computer is used to make a census map.

CHAPTER ✓ CHECKUP

Finish each sentence. Circle the letter in front of the correct answer.

1. Rules help you make choices and

   a. hurt people's feelings.
   b. know what is fair.
   c. count the population.
   d. read traffic lights.

2. You learn most rules from

   a. games, sports, homework.
   b. checkups, tickets, court.
   c. inspectors, safety, judges.
   d. family, friends, teachers.

3. A community's rules are called

   a. leaders.
   b. choices.
   c. laws.
   d. votes.

4. Many laws protect people's

   a. health and safety.
   b. census reports.
   c. languages and signs.
   d. food and feelings.

5. One example of a safety rule is

   a. throwing litter on the street.
   b. taking turns playing a game.
   c. obeying traffic signals.
   d. thanking someone for a gift.

6. If you break a law, you may have to

   a. make a new rule.
   b. pay a fine.
   c. visit a restaurant.
   d. go home.

Think of one rule in your community and explain why you think it is important.

_____

_____

_____

_____

_____

Communities Provide Services

You know that some workers provide services. Communities provide services, too. These services help people who live in communities. A school is one example of a service provided by a community.

Circle the person in the picture who is providing a service.

What Communities Need

Towns and cities need many services besides schools. All communities need a way to bring water and electricity to everyone who lives there. They need workers to put out fires and to protect people. Communities need roads and buildings, too.

Teachers are community workers.

84

How do communities provide services such as schools? They hire people to build them and work in them. It takes many people with many different skills to do all these jobs.

Look at the picture. Shade the hat of the worker who is hammering.

Circle the worker who is laying bricks.

Put an X on the worker who is putting in wires for electricity.

How Communities Pay for Things

Each person who works earns money. Workers pay part of the money they earn to their community. This payment is called a **tax**.

 Look at the flow chart below. Put a ✔ under the box that says WORKERS ARE PAID.

Circle the box about workers paying taxes.

The community spends tax money to build schools and to pay workers. Tax money helps the community to provide other services, too.

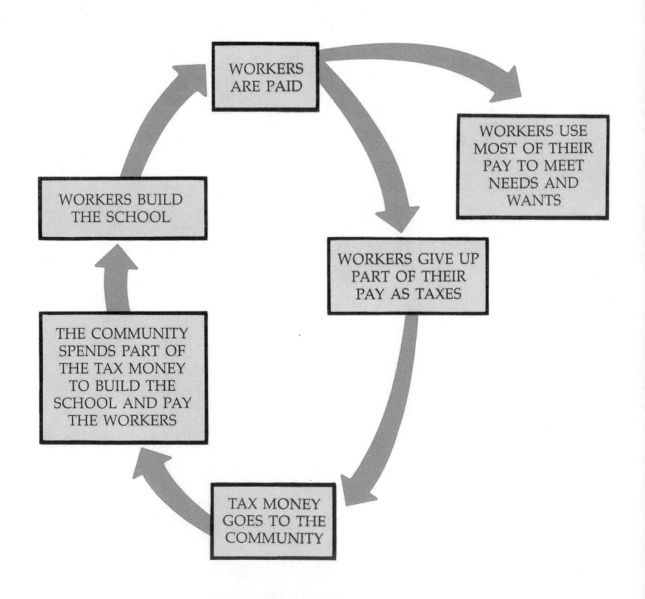

Hartsfield International Airport in Atlanta, Georgia, is one of the busiest airports in the United States.

Size and Services

A big community has lots of people working and living in it. So big cities collect more tax money than small towns. That is one reason why cities have paid firefighters instead of volunteers. That's also why big cities have more hospitals, large libraries and museums, and big airports. Cities also have more special services than you find in small communities.

What services does your community provide? Write two services in your community here.

_____

UNIT PROJECT Tip   Meet with your student planning team. Add to your list of ways to improve your school. This time, brainstorm the way you think tax money should be spent at your school. Pick your top three ideas.

Communities often provide special services. This community needs help clearing the snow. What kind of weather does your community have?

Sometimes communities, both large and small, need special services. Look at the picture to the left. What weather did this community have?

What service do the people of this community need when it snows? Write your answer here.

_____

Another service a community might offer is a consumer department. The workers in a consumer department make sure that consumers get what they pay for. Consumer workers check to see that store owners treat customers fairly.

The consumer worker in the picture below is checking prices in a drugstore.

How does this service help people in the community? Write your answer here.

_____

Communities often provide special services to protect consumers.

CHAPTER ✓ CHECKUP

Finish each sentence. Circle the letter in front of the correct answer.

1. Two services provided by communities are

   a. taxes and earnings.
   b. barbers and cleaners.
   c. schools and firefighting.
   d. students and teachers.

2. The payment that workers pay to a community is a

   a. gift.
   b. tax.
   c. want.
   d. service.

3. Workers use their money for

   a. libraries and museums.
   b. volunteer helpers.
   c. special services.
   d. needs, wants, taxes.

4. Small communities usually have

   a. less tax money than big cities.
   b. no tax money.
   c. more tax money than big cities.
   d. tax money only some years.

5. If shoppers think store owners are not fair, they can go to the

   a. health department.
   b. consumer department.
   c. weather department.
   d. fire department.

6. Many community services help

   a. cause problems.
   b. share problems.
   c. teach problems.
   d. solve problems.

 Imagine a town that did not collect taxes. What are three big problems that community would face? Write your answer here.

_____

_____

_____

_____

_____

Reading a Bar Graph

Look at the bar graph below. It shows the census count for the community of Olive Hill.

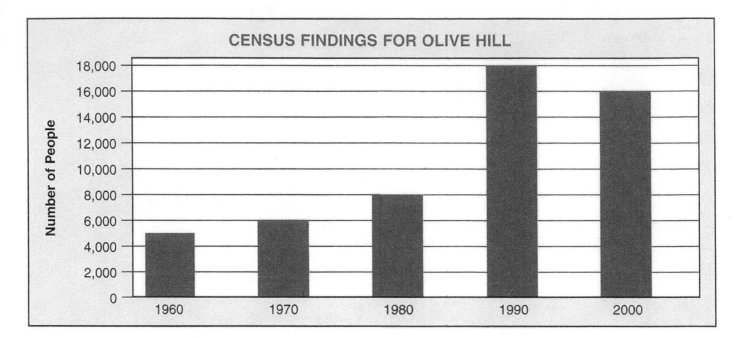

1. How many people lived in Olive Hill in 1960?

   _____

2. By what year had the number of people in Olive Hill grown to 18,000?

   _____

3. Were more people living in Olive Hill between 1980 and 1990 or between 1970 and 1980?

   _____

4. In 1995, a computer company opened in Bell Valley. Between 1995 and 2000, many people in Olive Hill moved to Bell Valley to work. How did this change the 2000 census?

   _____

Now it's time to finish your unit project. Think about what you learned about how communities are run. Talk with your team to answer questions like these.

- **How could you improve your school?**

- **What rules would make your school better?**

- **How should tax money be spent to improve your school?**

Decide how you want to share the information you gathered. Choose one of these ways or use one of your own ideas.

➤ Meet with your team. Look at your list of new rules and ways to spend tax money. Pick the most important idea in each list. Then combine your ideas with other teams' ideas. Write down each idea and put two boxes after it—one to vote *yes,* one to vote *no.* Before the vote, explain to the rest of the class why you think your ideas are good for the school.

➤ After the votes are counted, pick two winning ideas and make a bar graph showing how many people voted for and against each idea.

➤ Make election posters advertising a variety of ideas to improve the school. Include ideas for new rules and new ways to spend tax money.

Communities Change

Do you have a picture of yourself as a baby? You don't look much like that now! As you grow older, you'll change even more.

The same thing happens to communities. Omaha, Nebraska, changed. It is pictured here. Unit 5 will help you answer questions like these about how communities change.

- What were American Indian communities like long ago?

- How did pioneers start communities?

- What causes communities to change and grow?

UNIT PROJECT

Start a team project. Gather facts and pictures about your community's past and present. You will use this information to make a time line. Work on your project as you read Unit 5.

American Indian Communities

The land along the Missouri River is rich and good for farming. But in 1830, only about 2,000 people lived there. They were a group of American Indians called the Omaha. The map below shows where they lived.

The Omaha, like most people, liked living near each other. They lived in villages. Living close together made life safer from attacks.

 About how far was it across Omaha land? Write your answer here.

_____

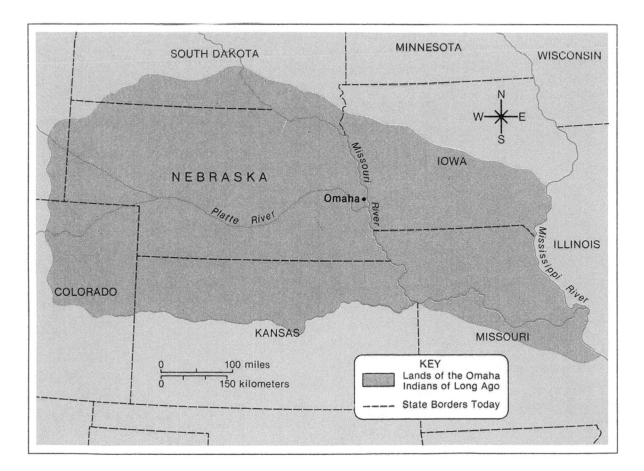

SOUTH DAKOTA

MINNESOTA

WISCONSIN

N
W—E
S

IOWA

NEBRASKA

Missouri River

Omaha•

Platte River

Mississippi River

ILLINOIS

COLORADO

KANSAS

MISSOURI

0   100 miles
0   150 kilometers

KEY
Lands of the Omaha
Indians of Long Ago
- - - - State Borders Today

The Omaha built their homes close together. They made them out of the earth itself. These homes were called **earth lodges.** Men and women worked together to make the earth lodges.

The first step was to outline the lodge walls in the dirt. One man did this job.

The man took a short, wooden pole and hammered it into the dirt. Then he tied a rope to the top of the pole. He pulled the rope tight. Holding onto the rope, he walked in a circle around the pole. The path he left showed where the wall would be. So he made sure he dragged and shuffled his feet!

Draw a line to finish the circle on the picture below.

After making the circle, a group of men cut heavy logs. The logs served as the frame for the house. The men hammered the logs into the ground along the marked path.

Look at the picture again. Where should the walls be put? Draw some lines to show where the men hammered logs to make the walls.

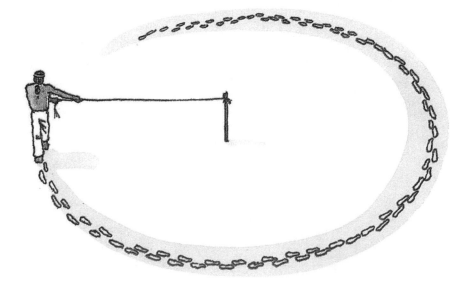

Once the walls were up, the women went to work. They dug out the center of the circle. That made the floor of the earth lodge lower than the land outside.

The women then cut blocks of soil. The soil was held together by grass and roots. The women pounded the blocks to make them flat. They used the blocks to make the roof.

How did men and women share the work of building the earth lodge?

_____

_____

Finally, the women dug a deep hole near the door. This hole was about eight feet deep. It was very wide at the bottom. But at the top, it was just wide enough to let a person down. The family stored food and clothing there for the winter. Look at the picture of the hole on the right.

Look at the bottom picture. Put an X where you could dig the hole to store food.

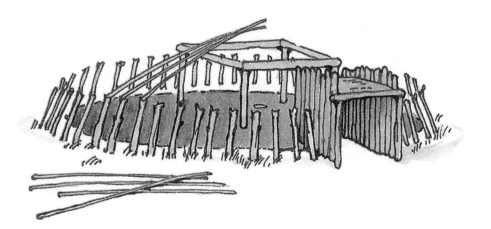

Look at the **diagram** of an Omaha village. A diagram is a drawing that shows how something works. Labels on the diagram explain the drawing.

This diagram shows how the Omaha lived. Omaha men, women, and children fished in the stream. Fields surrounded the village. Each family grew corn, beans, squash, and melons in its own field. Each family had horses, too. They were useful for hunting and traveling. Horses were very important to the Omaha.

 Draw a line under the label that tells you where the Omaha farmed.

Circle the label that tells you where the Omaha lived.

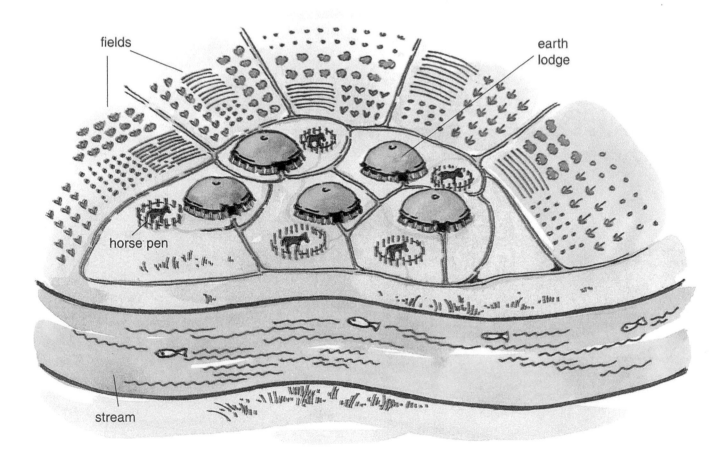

fields

earth lodge

horse pen

stream

Every June, the whole Omaha village changed. Almost everybody would leave! June was the time for the buffalo hunt.

Everyone went to hunt buffalo, except the old and the sick. Most villagers packed up and headed west. That's where the buffalo lived. They wandered the plains to the west.

The Omaha often had to travel many miles to find the buffalo. They took their bows and arrows and their cooking tools.

The Omaha hunted the buffalo for food. They used the skin to make **tepees.** Tepees were the tents that the Omaha lived in when they traveled. The tepees were easy to carry from one place to another.

Setting up the tepee was a woman's job. She made the tepee out of poles and buffalo skin.

Look at the drawing below. Circle the tepee.

The men went out to hunt the buffalo. When they saw the buffalo, they got on their horses. Sometimes the Omaha had to follow the buffalo for several days before they could get close enough to the buffalo. Then they quietly made a circle around the buffalo.

With screams and shouts, the hunters moved closer to the buffalo. The frightened animals ran in circles. This gave the hunters the chance to attack them with their bows and arrows.

 How did horses help the Omaha hunt? Write your answer here.

_____

_____

Then the women went to work on the buffalo. They were careful not to waste anything. They cut up all the meat and dried some for winter. They made clothes from the skin. The women also used the skin to make blankets and shoes.

The Omaha hunted buffalo all summer. By September, they returned to their villages. September was the time to pick the corn and other crops. It was the time to fish the streams. Crops and fish could be dried and stored for the winter.

The Omaha wondered what they would find when they got back. Would everything still be there? Would the crops still be in the fields? Or had they been stolen? When that happened, winter was very hard indeed. One way or another, the Omaha had to get ready for the cold months. It was time to go home.

What animals did the Omaha use to help them move? Circle them in the picture.

UNIT PROJECT Tip Work as a team to learn about American Indians who lived in your area. Find out the names of the groups and the dates they first came to the area. Draw pictures of their daily life.

Sequoyah

Do you know who the Cherokee are? They are a group of American Indians who lived in the southeastern United States. Sequoyah was a Cherokee who was born in 1760. He did something very important for his people. He made "talking leaves."

When Sequoyah was a little boy, the Cherokee had a spoken language but not a written language. Sequoyah learned new languages easily. He met many European settlers. He was interested in the way they wrote their languages.

Sequoyah spent 12 years finding a way to write his own language. Thanks to Sequoyah, many Cherokee learned to read and write their own language. They also published a newspaper and books. People called these written works "talking leaves."

Later in his life, Sequoyah went to Washington, D.C., to help American Indians. After he died, people named a park after him. They also named a kind of giant tree after him. No one will ever forget Sequoyah and his "talking leaves"!

Why do you think it was important for the Cherokee to have a written language? Write your answer here.

_____

_____

CHAPTER ✓ CHECKUP

Finish each sentence. Circle the letter in front of the correct answer.

1. The Omaha lived in what is now
   a. Florida.
   b. Nebraska.
   c. Oregon.
   d. New York.

2. An earth lodge is
   a. a community center.
   b. where the buffalo lived.
   c. what we live in today.
   d. a house that the Omaha used.

3. The Omaha used buffalo for
   a. food and clothing.
   b. traveling and sharing.
   c. pets and food.
   d. farm work.

4. In June, everyone left the Omaha villages to hunt buffalo except the
   a. women and babies.
   b. children and grandparents.
   c. old and sick.
   d. men and teenagers.

5. The Omaha lived near
   a. the Hudson River.
   b. the Nile River.
   c. the Missouri River.
   d. Niagara Falls.

6. The Omaha made tepees from
   a. buffalo skin.
   b. stone.
   c. cement.
   d. bricks.

 Why were the buffalo important to the Omaha? Write your answer here.

_____

_____

_____

_____

103

Early Communities

About 150 years ago, a new group of people came into Omaha land. They wanted land to farm. These people were called **pioneers** because they were among the first Americans to settle in this area.

 Look at the painting. Circle what the pioneers used for transportation.

The pioneers came west from St. Louis, Missouri, in the 1850s. At that time, there were about 100,000 people in St. Louis. There were only 2,000 in Omaha.

The pioneers took the Omaha land. They did not ask to use it. They just moved in. The Omaha knew they could not fight so many people. So they moved farther west.

In 1854, the pioneers started a town near the Missouri River. They named it after the Omaha who once lived there.

Omaha was a good place for a community. It was in the center of the country. Pioneers passed through Omaha on their way west. In Omaha, they bought things they needed.

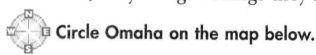 **Circle Omaha on the map below.**

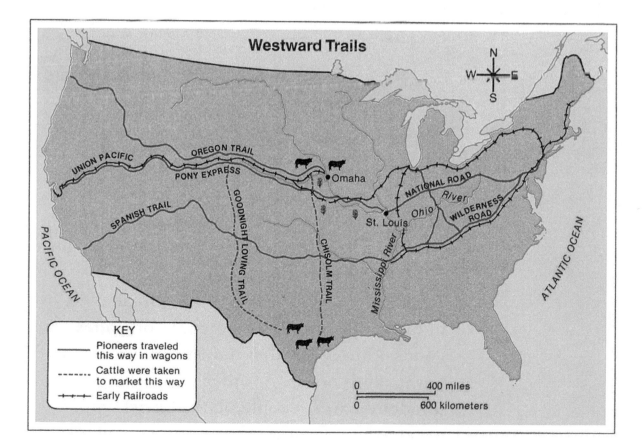

Early Omaha had many kinds of businesses.

Omaha was in the center of good farmland. The land was good for cattle, too. Cattle ranchers and farmers sold their goods in Omaha.

Look at the picture above. Circle a place where goods were sold.

There was plenty of water for the people of Omaha, because the Missouri River was so close. The Missouri was also good for transportation. Hundreds of steamboats traveled to and from Omaha every year. They carried goods and people.

Many new **industries** grew in Omaha. An industry is a business that makes or trades goods. One of the first industries in Omaha was making bricks. Another was making wooden boards. People needed bricks and wood to build houses.

In time, more people moved to Omaha and started new businesses. Then a railroad was built that crossed the entire United States. It went right through Omaha!

Look at the **time line** below. A time line shows a number of years. Marks on the line stand for things that happened. The time line shows events in the order that they happened. This time line shows important events in Omaha's early history.

THE EARLY HISTORY OF OMAHA

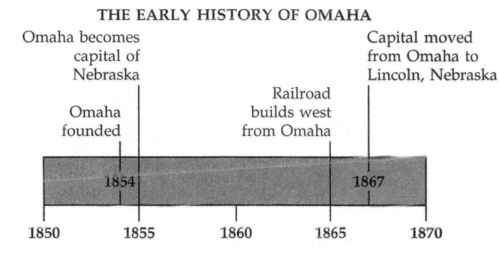

Omaha becomes capital of Nebraska

Capital moved from Omaha to Lincoln, Nebraska

Omaha founded

Railroad builds west from Omaha

1850   1854   1855   1860   1865   1867   1870

Look at the year Omaha was founded. How many years later was the railroad built?

The railroad helped Omaha grow. Trains brought cattle in from far away. Soon, new jobs opened in meat-packing, or getting meat ready to sell in other cities. Thousands of people came to Omaha for these jobs.

The trains also brought more corn and wheat from the farms. Mills were built to grind the corn and wheat into flour. The mills needed workers. So even more people came to Omaha to work in the mills.

Cattle were kept in pens near the railroad in Omaha.

Omaha's population grew quickly. New houses were built. New schools opened. So did a public library. Omaha grew from a tiny community into a busy city.

 Look at the map of Omaha. It has a grid, or lines that cross each other to form squares. Each square is named with a letter and number. Put your finger on the letter A. Follow it over to the column numbered 4. What is in A-4?

_____

 Color the Missouri River.

 Search for facts and pictures of your town's early years. What businesses started? When? What helped the town grow?

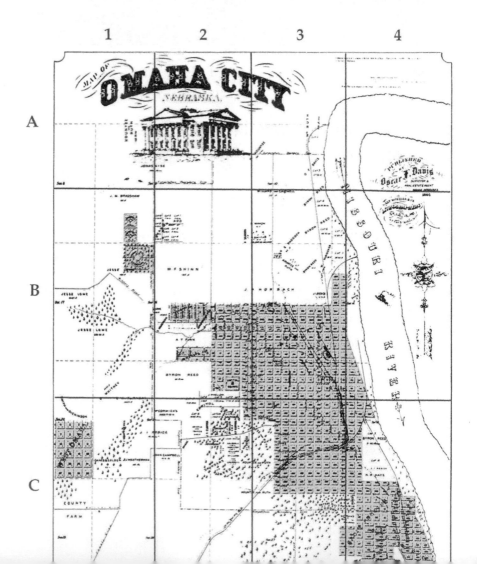

Do you know what a desert is? A desert is a place that gets very little rain. Crops such as corn and wheat cannot grow in a desert.

Omaha is in the state of Nebraska. Nebraska was once called part of the "Great American Desert." How did Nebraska get this name? In 1820, Army Major Stephen H. Long and his men explored this part of the country. Long reported that the land here was not good for farming. He called the land the "Great American Desert."

Because of what Major Long said, many pioneers did not try to farm in Nebraska. Most Americans traveled through Nebraska to places farther west.

When the first pioneers finally settled in Nebraska, they found that Major Long was wrong. The pioneers grew crops such as wheat and corn. Land that could not be farmed was good for feeding cattle.

Today, Nebraska is one of our country's most important farming states.

Farmers grow many different crops in Nebraska.

Major Long's report was wrong about Nebraska. Explain what made it wrong.

CHAPTER ✓ CHECKUP

Finish each sentence. Circle the letter in front of the correct answer.

1. The people who moved west long ago to find land are called
   a. Canadians.
   b. meat-packers.
   c. pioneers.
   d. New Yorkers.

2. Omaha is in the middle of
   a. the desert.
   b. the United States.
   c. the ocean.
   d. Texas.

3. People and goods traveled on the Missouri River in
   a. cars.
   b. trucks.
   c. steamboats.
   d. floats.

4. An industry is a business that
   a. makes or trades goods.
   b. provides services.
   c. is run by volunteers.
   d. was begun by the Omaha.

5. Bricks and wooden boards were needed in Omaha to build
   a. skyscrapers.
   b. houses.
   c. tepees.
   d. wagons.

6. In the 1800s, Omaha changed from a small community into a
   a. tiny village.
   b. busy city.
   c. town for American Indians.
   d. large state.

THINKING AND WRITING

How did the railroad help Omaha grow?

_____

_____

_____

_____

_____

110

Communities Grow

After 1880 Omaha kept growing. Today Omaha is Nebraska's biggest city. More than 390,000 people live there.

The city keeps growing because industry keeps growing. Preparing food is still Omaha's biggest industry. And Omaha is still a railroad center. But new industries and jobs have come to the city. These include computer work and selling goods by telephone.

Trucking is also a key industry. There are nearly 100 trucking businesses in Omaha. Trucking is an important way to move goods.

What is another way to move goods? Write your answer here.

Omaha, the largest city in Nebraska, is near the Missouri River.

111

Do you think there are people living in these houses?

As a city grows, it can have new problems. In parts of Omaha, some older buildings began to fall apart while other parts of the city grew. People began to move away from the older areas. As the people left, businesses in the area closed. Shoe repair shops, food stores, and other businesses could no longer make enough money. Finally, many buildings were left empty. The streets got dirty.

Look at the picture. What happens to a house when it is left empty? Write your answer here.

_____

_____

UNIT
PROJECT
Tip

Collect facts and pictures that show your community today. Have old areas been fixed up? Are new businesses moving in?

Today, people in Omaha are building new houses. Houses that are falling apart are being torn down to make room for the new homes.

In many parts of town, old buildings are being repaired. In one part of downtown Omaha, old warehouses have been fixed up. This area is called Old Market. Some old buildings have been turned into shops. Others have become restaurants. Now the old buildings are as good as new.

Look at the picture. Have these buildings been fixed? How can you tell? Write your answer here.

_____

_____

There are busy shops and places to eat in these old buildings.

113

Look at this map of Omaha. It shows the community in 1854, in 1880, and today. What changes do you see? What do you think will happen to Omaha in the **future**? The future means the years to come. Do you think that more people will live in Omaha? Or do you think that fewer people will live there? What changes could new kinds of transportation and industry bring?

 Look at the map. Name three ways in which Omaha has changed since 1854. Write your answer here.

_____

_____

_____

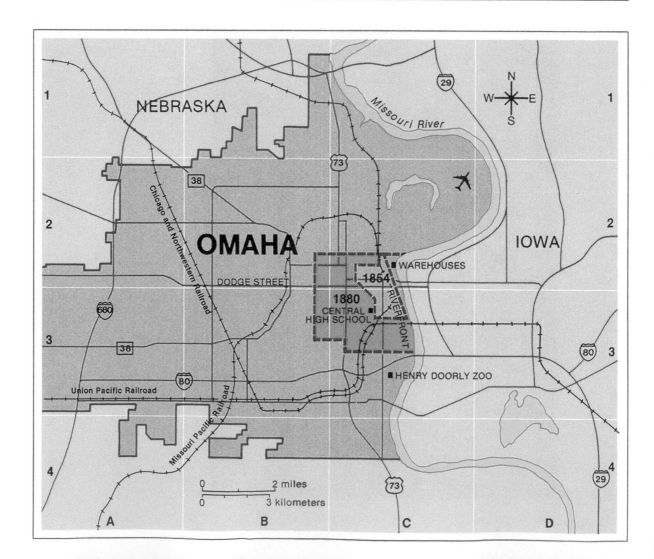

Look at the picture that shows Omaha just after it was settled. Then look at the picture of Omaha as it is today. What do you think Omaha's future will be like? Can you guess?

Name two things that are different between the Omaha of yesterday and the Omaha of today. Write your answer here.

_____

_____

Which Omaha would you rather live in? Omaha over 100 years ago? Or Omaha today?

An Aztec City

Mexico City has very old buildings right next to very new buildings.

Mexico City is the capital of Mexico. It has changed a lot over the years. It was once a city in the middle of a lake!

Long ago an American Indian group called the Aztecs built a city. This city was called Tenochtitlán. The city was built on an island in the middle of a lake. The Aztecs had plenty of water to grow food. But they did not have enough land. So they built islands of mud and plants. In time, most of the lake was turned into farmland. There was enough food for all the people. Soon Tenochtitlán became a huge city! It had canals, streets, gardens, and zoos.

People from Spain came to Tenochtitlán. They fought the Aztecs and took their city. The people from Spain built their own city where Tenochtitlán once stood. They called it Mexico City. After a few years, they completely drained the water from the lake. Now, Mexico City covers land where the lake used to be.

Look at the picture. There are ruins of old Aztec buildings in Mexico City. Some Spanish buildings still stand. But now the city has modern buildings, too. Millions of people live in Mexico City. Today, Mexico City is the world's second largest city!

Circle the Spanish church in the picture.

Put an X on a new building.

CHAPTER ✓ CHECKUP

Finish each sentence. Circle the letter in front of the correct answer.

1. Today Omaha is the biggest city in

   a. Kansas.
   b. Oklahoma.
   c. Texas.
   d. Nebraska.

2. Getting food ready for sale is

   a. not important in Omaha.
   b. the biggest industry in Omaha.
   c. not important anywhere.
   d. a very small business.

3. One industry that has grown in Omaha in the last 100 years is

   a. hunting buffalo.
   b. trucking.
   c. fishing.
   d. mills.

4. When people leave one part of a city, the houses there may

   a. look cleaner.
   b. start to fall apart.
   c. get crowded.
   d. become new.

5. Since 1854 Omaha has become

   a. empty.
   b. smaller.
   c. bigger.
   d. rural.

6. The future means

   a. past years.
   b. what is happening now.
   c. the years to come.
   d. what just happened.

Important jobs in Omaha include preparing food, computer work, and selling goods by telephone. Which job would you like the best? Explain your answer.

_____

_____

_____

_____

Unit 5 Skill Builder
Using a Diagram

Not all American Indian groups lived in communities like the Omaha. The Tlingit American Indians lived in southeastern Alaska. The diagram shows you how a Tlingit village looked.

totem pole

wooden canoes

1. The Tlingit used trees from nearby forests to build houses called plank houses. Find the line pointing to a plank house. Add the label "plank house."

2. Circle another thing the Tlingit made out of wood.

3. What two foods did the Tlingit eat?

   _____

4. The Tlingit carved animal pictures in tall tree trunks. What are these carvings called?

   _____

WOODMEN

Now it's time to finish your unit project. Think about what you learned about how communities change. Talk with your team about the answers to questions like these.

- **Who lived in your community long ago?**

- **When did the first businesses open?**

- **How did your community grow?**

- **What important things happened in your community this year? Last year?**

Decide how you want to show the information you gathered. Choose one of these ways or use one of your own ideas.

➤ Meet with your team. Review the material you collected about your community. Then choose the most important events in your community's past. Use these events to make a time line. Illustrate your time line with the pictures you drew and collected.

➤ Use your facts and pictures to make a book about your community for a time capsule. Explain what caused your community to change.

➤ Use your pictures and information to make a bulletin board display. Call your bulletin board "How Our Community Changed."

UNIT 6

Communities Share

Each community in the United States is different. And each is special in its own way.

Communities in the United States also share many things. Most important, they are all part of one nation.

Unit 6 will help you find answers to questions like these about the things all American communities share.

- What community do we all share?
- What traditions do we all celebrate?

Start a team project. Make a collection of objects and pictures of things made in the United States. Work on your project as you read this unit.

Our Nation's Capital

One community that is important to all Americans is Washington, D.C. Washington is the capital of the United States. D.C. stands for the District of Columbia. It is land that is set aside for the nation's capital. Washington, D.C., is not part of any state.

A City of Government

The government of the United States meets in Washington, D.C. This government is called the national government. The leader of the national government is the President. The picture below shows the White House where the President lives.

Why do you think the President lives in such a big house? Write your answer here.

_____

The President lives and works in the White House.

The Capitol building is also in Washington. It's the big building in the center of the picture below. Lawmakers from all the states meet in this building.

Like the lawmakers who are part of community government, these lawmakers are **elected.** To elect someone means to choose that person by voting. Lawmakers are elected by the people who live in their state.

All the lawmakers elected by the states meet and work together in the Capitol. This group of lawmakers is called **Congress.**

Write *Capitol* on the picture next to the Capitol.

Next to the picture, write the name of the group that meets in the Capitol.

The Capitol is one of the most famous buildings in Washington.

The Supreme Court building is near the Capitol in Washington, D.C. You can see it in the picture on page 122. It is the white building on the left behind the Capitol.

The **Supreme Court** judges meet here. (Remember that a court is where a judge works.) The Supreme Court is the most important court in our country. It decides things about our nation's laws. Everyone must follow what the Supreme Court judges decide about our laws.

The President, Congress, and Supreme Court form the three branches, or parts of our government. The chart shows these parts. A chart shows information in a way that is easy to read.

Underline the part of government that makes laws that all states have to follow.

Circle the part of government that leads the government.

Put an X on the part of government that decides if national laws are broken.

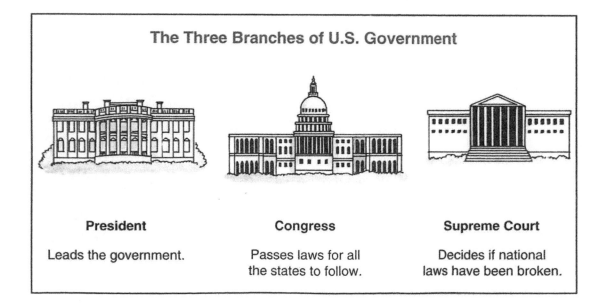

The Three Branches of U.S. Government

President	Congress	Supreme Court
Leads the government.	Passes laws for all the states to follow.	Decides if national laws have been broken.

The statue of Abraham Lincoln is in the Lincoln Memorial.

How did Washington, D.C., get its name? That's easy! It was named after George Washington, the first President of the United States.

The picture shows a statue of another President. His name was Abraham Lincoln. Lincoln was one of our most important Presidents. He was the President who ended slavery.

Why do you think Lincoln looks so serious? Write your answer here.

_____

Washington has many beautiful statues of Presidents. It also has many statues that honor people who fought in wars.

Washington has many other interesting places that are important to all Americans. Do you like books? One of the world's largest libraries is in Washington, D.C. It is called the Library of Congress.

Washington is also home to a very famous museum. Its name is the Smithsonian Institution. But its nickname is "the nation's attic." This museum is made up of eight museums. Together they hold many treasures that belong to all Americans. Among these treasures are toys and games used by American children long ago. The museums also hold the first airplane and the spacecraft that went to the moon!

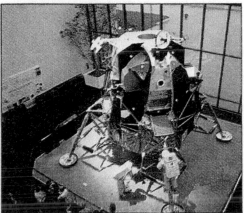

Why do you think the things shown here should be stored in Washington, D.C.?

_____

_____

(above) The National Air and Space Museum, part of the Smithsonian Institution, has exhibits on U.S. air and space flights. (left) This is the original building of the Smithsonian Institution. Nicknamed "the castle," it is now the location of the institution's main offices.

UNIT PROJECT Tip With your team, search for pictures of machines, quilts, art, balls, bats, and other things used in sports, clothing—even food—made in the United States.

Sandra Day O'Connor

Supreme Court Justice Sandra Day O'Connor

Nine judges make up the Supreme Court. These judges are called justices. The justices are chosen for the job by the President. Once chosen, they serve on the court for the rest of their lives.

Until 1981 every Supreme Court judge in our history was a man. But in that year, Sandra Day O'Connor became the first woman Supreme Court justice. For the first time in 192 years, a woman served on the Supreme Court.

O'Connor was born in El Paso, Texas. She went to school there. Later, she went to law school, where she was a top student.

After law school, O'Connor had a hard time getting work. In the 1950s most lawyers were men. Many people thought that being a lawyer was too hard a job for women. In time, O'Connor found work as a lawyer in California and in Arizona. Later, she became a lawmaker and then a judge. People saw that she worked hard. They saw that she was clear thinking and fair.

President Ronald Reagan chose O'Connor to be a Supreme Court justice. On April 20, 1995, she became the first woman to run a Supreme Court meeting.

In what year did Sandra Day O'Connor join the Court? Write your answer here.

_____

CHAPTER ✓ CHECKUP

Finish each sentence. Circle the letter in front of the correct answer.

1. The District of Columbia is
   a. part of another country.
   b. the name of a U.S. state.
   c. an area for the U.S. capital.
   d. the highest court in the land.

2. The White House is where
   a. people in Congress work.
   b. the President lives and works.
   c. old American things are kept.
   d. the Supreme Court meets.

3. Congress meets in the
   a. Supreme Court building.
   b. Capitol building.
   c. Lincoln Memorial.
   d. Smithsonian Institution.

4. Elected means
   a. serves for life.
   b. chosen by the President.
   c. chosen by a vote.
   d. ruled by law.

5. The Supreme Court decides
   a. if national laws are broken.
   b. where to put statues.
   c. who will be President.
   d. what money to print.

6. The national government is made up of
   a. two parts.
   b. four parts.
   c. eight parts.
   d. three parts.

THINKING AND WRITING How are the national government and community governments alike? Write your answer here.

_____

_____

_____

_____

_____

Communities Celebrate

American communities **celebrate** many of the same **holidays**. To celebrate means to remember an important day or event in a special way. Can you think of some holidays you celebrate with your family?

National Holidays

Each year in November, people in every city and town in the United States sit down to a big dinner. This is a holiday Americans call Thanksgiving.

The first Thanksgiving was held in 1621 by Pilgrims who were new to this land. They gave thanks for good crops and for being alive.

Look at the picture. What are two foods the Pilgrims served? Write your answer here.

_____

_____

Some of the people at the first Thanksgiving were friendly neighbors. They included an American Indian chief and many other American Indians. They had helped the Pilgrims stay alive.

The American Indians taught the Pilgrims how to grow corn. They showed them how to fish with a spear.

The idea of spending a holiday together became an American **tradition.** A tradition is something people do in the same way that has been passed down over many years.

In 1863, President Abraham Lincoln made Thanksgiving more than a tradition. He made it a national holiday for everyone in the United States.

How is your celebration different from the Thanksgiving in the picture below? Write your answer here.

_____

PROJECT Tip Gather material about national holiday celebrations. Collect facts about traditions that groups of Americans celebrate, such as Chinese New Year or Hannukah.

These children are taking part in a hometown parade.

On July 4, 1776, another American tradition began. On that day the United States became a free nation. It was no longer ruled by Great Britain. People celebrated with meetings, parades, and parties. Today this holiday is known as the Fourth of July. Many communities celebrate our nation's birthday with fireworks and parades. Their celebrations honor our freedoms.

The flag is an important part of the Fourth of July celebration. The American flag has 50 stars, one for each state. In this way, the flag stands for the fact that we are a single nation made up of many states.

Look at the picture. Circle the American flags.

Why do you think this might be a Fourth of July parade?

_____

_____

Celebrating Kwanzaa

In 1966, a college teacher named Dr. Maulana Karenga started a new holiday called *Kwanzaa*. He wanted to teach African Americans about their African traditions.

Dr. Karenga went to Africa and learned that many African people celebrate the first harvest of the year. This celebration is called *matunda ya kwanza*, which means "the first fruits." The words are in Swahili, an East African language. Dr. Karenga started Kwanzaa based on this festival and other traditions from Africa. Part of Kwanzaa honors seven rules for African American life. These include *Nia*, which says that African Americans should work to make their people great.

African Americans celebrate Kwanzaa from December 26 to January 1. Each day honors one of the rules. Family members gather and light one candle each evening. Then they talk about the rule for the day. Many families exchange homemade gifts. Near the end of the holiday, people of the community have a special dinner called *karamu*. At *karamu* people wear African clothing, eat traditional African foods, and enjoy music and dancing.

Lighting candles is part of the way families celebrate Kwanzaa.

Think of a rule for life you think would be good for all Americans. Write your answer here.

_____

_____

CHAPTER ✓ CHECKUP

Finish each sentence. Circle the letter in front of the correct answer.

1. The Pilgrims held Thanksgiving so they could

   a. help the American Indians.
   b. start an American tradition.
   c. get to know their neighbors better.
   d. give thanks for good crops.

2. Something people do in the same way that has been passed down over many years is

   a. a parade.
   b. a holiday.
   c. a tradition.
   d. a celebration.

3. President Lincoln made Thanksgiving a

   a. national tradition.
   b. national holiday.
   c. friendly meal.
   d. national birthday.

4. The Fourth of July celebrates

   a. parties and parades.
   b. the parades of 1776.
   c. Chinese New Year.
   d. our nation's birthday.

5. Two things that can be part of your own family's tradition are

   a. language and holidays.
   b. animals and television.
   c. harvests and dragons.
   d. parents and meetings.

6. A fiesta is a

   a. holiday.
   b. poem.
   c. parade.
   d. meeting.

How do national places and holidays help us feel like Americans? Write your answer here.

_____

_____

_____

Using a Chart

Did you know that there are thousands of celebrations and festivals in our country? Look at the chart below to find out when, where, why, and how some other communities celebrate.

Community Celebrations			
Kōloa Plantation Days	**Chasco Fiesta**	**Tulip Festival**	**Cherry Festival**
When? July	March	April	July
Where? Kōloa town, Kaua'i, Hawaii	New Port Richey, Florida	Owensville, Missouri	Traverse City, Michigan
Why? Celebrates the first planting in the late 1800s of sugar crops in Hawaii	Celebrates the friendship of Calusa Indians and Spanish settlers	Celebrates the beginning of spring	Celebrates that the area's cherry crops are ripe and ready for eating
How? A parade, games, and a car show	Games, dances, and food	A quilt show, a dance, and a flower show	A parade, pie-eating contest, music, and the crowning of the National Cherry Queen

1. Which celebration is about friendship?

   _____

2. What festival could you see in Missouri in April?

   _____

3. What community would you be in if you entered a cherry pie-eating contest?

   _____

4. Which two celebrations honor crops?

   _____

Now it's time to finish your project. Think about what you've learned about communities in the United States. Talk with your team about answers to questions like these.

- **What different things are made in the United States?**

- **What celebrations do Americans share?**

- **What celebrations make our country interesting?**

Decide how you want to show the information you gathered. Choose one of these ways or use one of your own ideas.

➤ Meet with your team. Look through the pictures and objects you collected. Pick the best ones and use them to make a museum display. You might want to arrange things by subject, like machines or celebrations. Or you might want to make a quilt design with your pictures. Give your display a title.

➤ Make a collage of your objects and pictures. Ask your school principal to display your collage in the library or hall.

➤ Make a book called *Made in the U.S.A.* Put the pictures you collected in the book and write a sentence about each of the pictures. Ask your school librarian to display your book in the library.

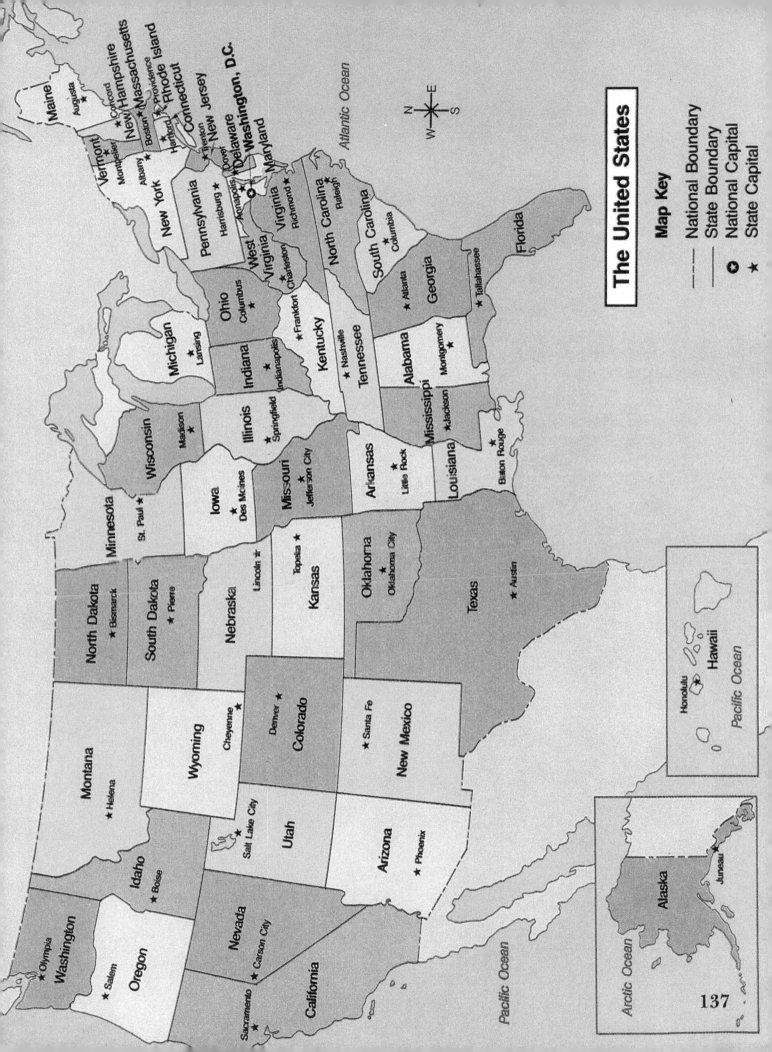

The United States

Map Key

- — — National Boundary
- —— State Boundary
- ✪ National Capital
- ★ State Capital

137

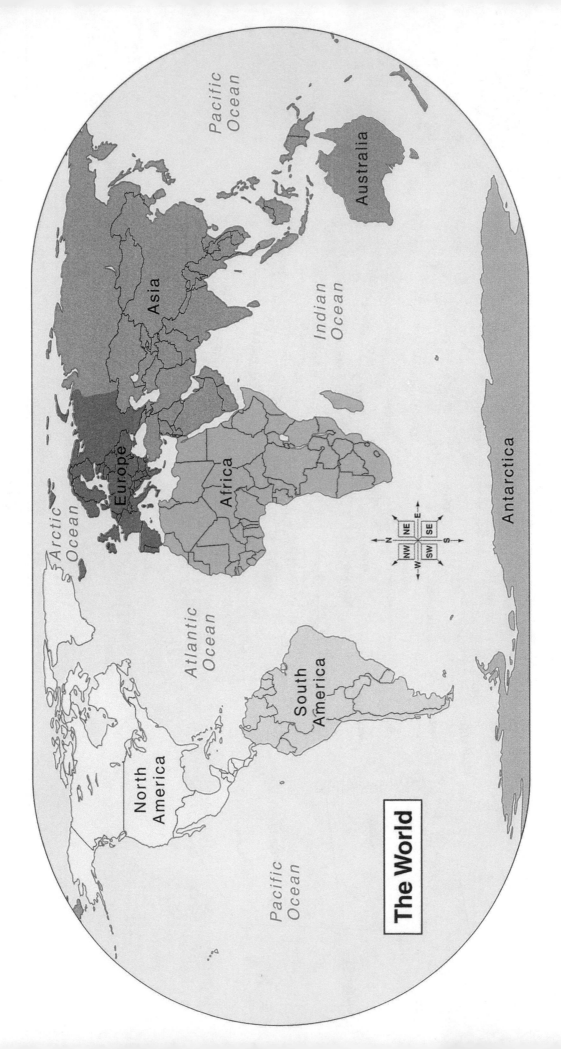

The World

Glossary

address (page 44) An address tells where a person lives.

bar graph (page 72) A bar graph uses bars to stand for numbers. It helps you compare different groups of numbers.

border (page 44) A border is a line on a map that shows where one place ends and another place begins.

business (page 10) A business is a store or other place where things are bought or sold.

canyon (page 19) A canyon is a very deep valley with steep walls.

capital (page 7) A capital is the city where the leaders of a government meet.

celebrate (page 128) To celebrate means to remember an important day or event in a special way. People often celebrate on holidays, such as July 4.

census (page 82) A census is a count of how many people live in a place.

chart (page 74) A chart presents facts in a way that is easy to read.

climate (page 17) Climate is the kind of weather a place has over time.

community (page 6) A community is a place where people live, work, and play.

compass rose (page 7) A compass rose shows directions on a map.

Congress (page 122) Congress is the group of people who make the nation's laws.

consumer (page 54) A consumer is a person who buys something to eat or to use.

depend on (page 9) To depend on something means to put your trust in it.

diagram (page 98) A diagram is a drawing that shows how something works. Labels on the diagram explain the drawing.

distance scale (page 8) A distance scale is a measuring line on a map. It helps people find distances.

dock (page 25) A dock is a platform built over water. Boats load and unload at a dock.

earth lodge (page 96) An earth lodge was a home built of earth by the Omaha people, a group of American Indians.

elect (page 122) To elect someone means to choose a person by voting. People elect the President every four years.

factory (page 39) A factory is a building or a group of buildings where things are made. Cars are made in factories.

fiesta (page 132) *Fiesta* is the Spanish word for "holiday."

flow chart (page 62) A flow chart is a diagram that shows the step-by-step order in which something is done.

future (page 114) The future means the time that is to come.

globe (page 65) A globe is a round model of Earth.

goods (page 39) Goods are things that are made to be sold like shoes or toys.

government (page 73) A government is a group of leaders who make laws.

grid (page 108) A grid is a group of lines that cross each other to form squares. Each square is named with a letter and number.

harbor (page 38) A harbor is an area of water that is protected from wind and strong waves. It is a safe place for ships.

industry (page 106) An industry is a business that makes or trades goods.

judge (page 73) A judge decides if a law has been broken.

landform (page 18) A landform is a shape of the land, such as a mountain or a hill.

law (page 73) A law is a rule made by a government.

lawmakers (page 73) Lawmakers are people who make new laws and change old ones.

map key (page 7) A map key tells about each symbol on a map. It tells what each symbol stands for.

mayor (page 73) A mayor is a person who leads a community.

mineral (page 16) A mineral is something made by nature that you can usually find in the earth in rocks.

mountain (page 18) A mountain is very high land.

natural resource (page 15) A natural resource is something from nature that people need and use. Water and trees are natural resources.

needs (page 53) Needs are things people must have in order to live.

pioneer (page 104) A pioneer is a person who goes to live in a new place. Many pioneers went west to farm the land.

plain (page 18) A plain is flat land.

political map (page 44) A political map of the United States shows states and their borders.

population (page 27) Population is the number of people living in a place.

producer (page 54) A producer is someone who gets paid for growing or for making something.

public (page 11) A public place is a place for everyone to use.

rural (page 27) A rural area is in the country. Farms are found in rural areas.

service (page 55) A service is something people do that other people need or want.

shelter (page 53) Shelter is a home or a place to live.

slave (page 48) A slave is a person who is owned by another person.

suburb (page 31) A suburb is a community near a big city.

Supreme Court (page 123) The Supreme Court is the most important court in the nation.

symbol (page 7) A symbol is found on a map. A symbol stands for a real thing.

tax (page 86) A tax is money that people pay to the government.

tepee (page 99) A tepee was a tent made from buffalo skin. The Omaha people lived in tepees when they traveled hunting buffalo.

time line (page 107) A time line shows a number of years. Marks on the line stand for things that happened. It shows the order in which they happened.

tradition (page 129) A tradition is something people do in the same way that has been passed down over many years.

transportation (page 33) Transportation is how people or things get from one place to another.

valley (page 19) A valley is the low land between hills or mountains.

volunteer (page 28) A volunteer is a person who is not paid for his or her work.

wants (page 53) Wants are things people would like but do not need to have in order to live.

weather (page 14) Weather is how hot or cold and how wet or dry it is.

Index

4500809918-0607-2020

Printed in the U.S.A